Chronicles and Narratives

Chronicles and Narratives

Tales from Strawberry Plains & Gay Street

p smith

Crippled Beagle Publishing
Knoxville, Tennessee, USA
www.crippledbeaglepublishing.com

Cover design by Robin Easter
Cover artwork by Kevin Armstrong

Paperback ISBN 978-1-965334-21-8
Hardcover ISBN 978-1-965334-22-5

Library of Congress Control Number: 2024923058

Printed in the United States of America

The Author's Disclaimer:
I'm eighty-four years old and a storyteller creating a legacy book for family and friends. I couldn't track down all the people pictured here because, honestly, most of them are dead. So, I'm asking forgiveness vs. permission, which is kind of how I've lived my life anyway. Cheers!

TO NANCY VALA, my mentor, who suggested I write down some of my stories...who read them, gently made corrections but allowed me write as I speak. Thank you, Nancy. Long day done.

Contents

Foreword

When Patti Smith tells a story, she purposefully describes each character—and always only in the first person. I used to listen to her stories and think, "I don't know who you are talking about!" But I soon came to realize that by the end of the story, I did. Patti is a consummate storyteller. She brings you into the lives and adventure of others in ways that make you feel like you were always along for the ride. Of course, you don't need to know a last name. You know these people!

I met Patti nearly forty years ago when she owned a sign shop in the fledgling Old City. It seemed like such an odd place for a shop…to everyone but Patti. The Old City was thirty miles and a world apart from the rambling farmhouse in Strawberry Plains and life she had as a county teacher, but it offered the friendships and adventure that fuel Patti. It was the beginning of her twenty-plus years as a downtown entrepreneur, activist, social coordinator, and megaphone vocalist. It was the source of the lifetime of adventures she has chronicled in this book.

Patti will remind you that she's a storyteller, not a writer. But I know you'll be grateful that she picked up a pencil to bring these tales to you. Enjoy the ride! —Carol Evans

Introduction

Why am I writing? I was retired when COVID hit but I had been working as an Uber driver and a track and field official. I was afraid to drive, and all track meets were canceled. A friend suggested that I write down some of the stories I had told her, so I did. As I wrote, the writing triggered other memories and off I would go into other parts of my life. I was born in 1940, so I had a very large number of years to travel. This writing was for my boys but then it became fun to remember people I knew, places I had gone and events which shaped my life. Most people would not tell a lot of stuff that happens to them, but I figure not telling does not mean it did not happen......so I am waiting for next......what next?......I do not know, but I am ready for it....whatever *next* is. I hope that in reading this you will remember long ago, forgotten people and places that were so important to your life.

Family

Son Solon, grandson Seth, and son Adam

To the Boys

Boys, this is something I figured out a long time ago. Life is about making Choices. You can Choose to hang on or let go ---You can Choose to roll with it or get rolled over by it. You can Choose to keep it or let it go. As you travel through your life, you keep each little hurt, each insult and anything you perceive that was bad done to you or you Choose to let it go.

Picture this: You are moving through your life with a big sack over your shoulder and each hurt is represented by a River Rock. You pick up the River Rock and put it in the sack over your shoulder. After you have traveled enough distance, picked up enough rocks and carried them, the weight of the rocks will bend you over until all you can see is the space between your feet.

You have lost your forward vision and no longer can stand tall. Let the Rocks go......let the Hurts go. As you let go of each Rock your load becomes lighter and easier to carry.

Look ahead, stand strong and tall....... YOUR CHOICE. I learned this many years ago by looking in the mirror and this is what the mirror said to me.

McPeter's Thanksgiving, 2021 at Amanda and Gary Sharpe's

Helma's

Courage is fostered by necessity. In 1942, my mother, Wilhelmina (Helma) Lenora Neubert McPeters was newly widowed with a sixth-grade education and three small children. She worked the night shift at a nearby factory, planted a garden, and sewed our clothes, even our winter coats. In 1947 she bought a grocery store, then a grill and after that she built a restaurant. She introduced catering and buffets to East Knox County. By the time she retired in 1988, Helma's had become a landmark in East Tennessee.

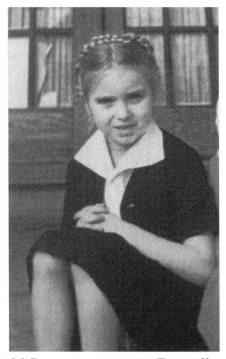

Patti McPeters, age seven in Trentville, 1947

Helma knew nothing about owning a food-service business; she liked to cook and was good at it. The restaurant started out with six counter stools, two tables and three booths. She would open the doors to fishermen waiting for an early morning breakfast. She served sandwiches and later added plate lunches. Later the restaurant added curb service, a small back porch which turned into a larger one and a small garden with tables. "Never one to sit quietly by while a bee buzzed in her bonnet." – Barbara Aston-Wash, Knoxville News-Sentinel.

Helma's Original Grill

She was six years old in 1914 and living with her Aunt Lenary on Strawberry Plains Pike in the Ramsey Community. Aunt Lenary taught her to cook, sew, make garden, and sell eggs. The only way to get the eggs to market in Knoxville was by use of the family buggy. From this early education she developed the skills for rearing a family and owning a restaurant that would become a landmark. Her life's progression was wife, mother, factory assembly line worker, grocery store owner, grill owner and restaurant owner. How could a forty-year-old widow with three children build this?

In 1959, a big brick building was built to house the 10,000-square-foot restaurant. Later banquet rooms were added upstairs and down along with a second kitchen used for banquets and catering. Helma's buffet was the first in the area. She charged $1.50 for adults and a special price for children. The buffet table was four, 2'x 6' folding tables covered in a lace tablecloth she had sewed. All the food was in glass bowls except for the hot food, which was in chaffing pans with canned heat. The buffet became so popular that on Sunday there would be a line out the door and travelers would drive out of their way to eat there. She added a breakfast buffet in 1971.

Restaurant

One interesting item that was included in the new building was a small "jute-box" at each booth in the dining room. A new sign was installed at the intersection of highways 11E and 11W on Asheville Highway and was used as a directional. Go to Helma's and go straight to Dandridge or bear left to go to Jefferson City. There must be something special about Helma's Sign. She sold the business in 1988 and there have been several owners but the sign is still there.

At the beginning of Integration, she was asked, "Miss Helma, you are not going to serve those black people here, are you?" She replied, "No, not unless they have money." She had a way of quietly leading. I never remember her raising her voice——ever. At work you could always tell when she was upset because she would go through the downstairs kitchen picking up and banging down pots and pans, but she never raised her voice.

Helma was the first to offer catering in the Knoxville area. She bought a van, hot and cold boxes, and insulated urns for transporting food and drink. Her friends who owned Regas, Buddies, and other restaurants wanted to get into the catering business, but had no equipment, so she would lend them what they needed. Friends helping friends. She catered to two movie sets, "Fool Killer" with Tony Perkins and "All the Way Home" with Robert Preston and Jean Simmons. In the summer of 1963, I had just graduated from the University of Tennessee and had been hired for my first teaching job at Gulf Park College to begin in the fall. That summer I worked catering with her.

Helma's Original Buffet

One day we were on the way to a remote location in a cow pasture in Blount County when she drove through a construction site. There was a big drop-off, and it jarred open the hot box door and two pans of vegetables fell out. She always had more food than she needed to cover any emergency, thank goodness. Another time, and this was totally my fault, we had arrived and had everything set up when I realized I had forgotten the flatware. This was a true panic so I drove every little backroad I could find and stopped at any kind of store until I had bought enough to get us through the meal. She loved Mr. Preston, and she said, "everybody did."

When he was co-starring with Mary Martin in "I Do, I Do" in New York she went to see the play and Mr. Preston invited her backstage. Her friends thought she was going to embarrass them all by wanting to go backstage but when Mr. Preston saw her, he threw open his arms for a big hug and in a loud voice said, "Helma." She catered all over East Tennessee and the largest party she ever catered was to 5,300 people at the Magnavox Factory in Morristown, Tennessee. There were two menus. One for adults, which was fried chicken, vegetables, salads, bread and dessert and one for the children that was hot dogs, hamburgers and cookies. I worked that party, and it was a mountain of food and a whole town of people. Thank goodness it was summer, and we were outside.

She was active in professional organizations. In 1966, she was President of the Knoxville Restaurant Association and served on the Better Business Board of Directors from 1977-1983. Because of her dedication to the restaurant business she was honored in 1977 as Tennessee Restauranteur of the year and was inducted into the Hall of Fame. Later she was invited to Florida State University to speak to the School of Culinary Arts.

She loved the beach and anytime we went on vacation we went to Daytona Beach, Florida. The first several vacations we stayed in cabins on the beach. Family and friends joined us, and we would go on deep sea fishing trips, but the adult's favorite nighttime entertainment was the Dog Races.

When they were out at night, I oversaw the three younger children…I was twelve. We would be dropped off at the Boardwalk and they would pick us up on the way back to the cabins. One night they forgot to pick us up. We sat on the curb waiting until a police officer saw us and I explained our dilemma. Keep in mind this way before cell phones. The officer took us home and waited until we were safely in somebody's care.

Patti and Helma clean tables after a catering party (photo courtesy of Beverly Duncan Gleason).

One trip on the way to Daytona we drove through the old part of Saint Augustine. The streets were very narrow, two cars could barely pass, and we met a car coming toward us. I will never forget the woman driver. She had rings on all her fingers, and she was holding a cigarette. Just as we came window to window with the woman she said to my stepfather, "don't you know this is one way?" his reply, which I will never forget, was "Hell, lady I am just going one way."

The women loved the auctions held at the boardwalk and they bought "things" .... lots of "things." My Mom loved the beach but was deathly afraid of the water. One morning several of us were standing knee deep in the water when a wave knocked us down. My Mom grabbed both my ankles and held on for dear life; however, my head was under water, but she saved me. After several years of renting places, she bought a house on the beach in Ponce Inlet, which is the last neighborhood before the Inlet. My brother, sister and I all loved taking our families there when they were young and to this day is my "Happy Place" even though we no longer own it.

She was fearless. She was married in 1928 and wanted to learn to drive. My dad would not teach her, so one day while he was at work, she taught herself. My Dad found out quickly what she had done because everybody in the small rural community told him. She had been driving, all day, on the wrong side of the road.

Once in Memphis, she was attending the Tennessee Restaurant Convention and wanted to meet Elvis. She drove to Graceland and the gate was open, so she drove up and parked at the front door. She knocked on the door and when it was opened, she was informed, tersely, that "Mr. Presley was not in residence," but she could truthfully say that she went to visit Elvis, but he was not at home.

In 1962 she married Roy Gilreath. He was a quiet man who allowed Helma to be Helma without interference. After they moved into the big house they developed a routine. She would leave the restaurant at 11:00 p.m. and would call him as she was leaving. He would open the electronic gate at the bottom of the driveway, just off the four-lane, so that when she turned into the driveway she would not have to stop. One night someone had jimmied the gate, and it was only half open, so she had to stop. When she did, a man stepped up, put a pistol up to her window, jerked her out of the car and took her purse. She had never learned to "cuss", so she stood outside the car yelling at the thief "Run you Sun Bitch my husband is on his way with a gun."

She was not much of a smoker or drinker. She had two cigarettes a day. One day at 3:00 p.m. when she came home for a nap and the other when she got off work at eleven. I do not remember her having a drink at home. She only drank white wine.

One time the whole family gathered in Baltimore for my niece's wedding. The wedding was a lavish affair held in The Baltimore Basilica. Kelli and Billy, the bride and groom, were transported to the reception at the country club in Hank's Bentley. Hank was my brother's friend who owned the hotel on the Harbor where we were staying. At the reception there were two food tables and a large band. We got there before most of the guest arrived and were seated on a glassed-in porch with large round tables. I asked Mom if she would like a glass of wine. I do not remember her eating much but she did drink wine through-out the evening. Hank walked us out to the station wagon to return to the hotel.

Brad, my nephew, who was driving and my son, Solon, were in the front seat. Mom and I sat in the middle of the back seat, holding hands and laughing at everything. Light poles, crosswalks, everything was funny.

Patti, Helma, and Doug in 1963, New Orleans

Arrowhead was built it 1966. It overlooked Douglas Lake and into the mountains and was built for family, friends and parties.... of course. It was shaped like an arrow. The arrowhead was the living room with all floor- to- ceiling windows and the shaft (the long part of the house) had four bedrooms and two baths. There was a kitchen, but the screened-in porch was all Helma. She installed a commercial grill for big breakfasts of pancakes, bacon, ham and eggs or later in the day - hamburgers or grilled cheese sandwiches. There was a boat and a tennis court. It became known as a "lover's lane" because when nobody was there a vehicle could be secluded. Sometimes the intruders would set-off the alarm, but nobody was ever caught.

My Mom taught us how to keep peace in the family. She and my sister, Jean, had gone up to Arrowhead and found the door to the freezer standing open. It had been open for days...what a mess. Mom said "who in the world left the door open?" My sister said "Patti." I was living in Mississippi and had not been home for weeks but this way nobody got their feelings hurt. Also, they discovered that the clothes dryer had caused a button to fall off the freezer and lodge in the door.

The "Big House", or Gilreath Manor, was a three floor English Tudor with four garages that sat on a hill in the middle of one-hundred acres overlooking the Holston River. She had four garages; none were used to house her car. There was a three bay for yard equipment and a double garage attached to the house. This was never used for her car because she stored her canned goods along the wall and a big table sat in the middle of the space for food service for parties. Her car sat in the cold, rain, wind and ice.

She had a big electric pump organ in the Sunroom. The Sunroom is not just a Sunroom, it is the Special View Room. When the house was being built, there was the big hole in the front wall, and she would stand and enjoy the view of the hills and Holston River. The big hole was for the fireplace and when all the stone was installed, she lost "her view." She had a three-hundred guest party to welcome her friends to her new home on a Sunday and on Monday out came the window at the side of the living room and construction began on the Sunroom so she could have a view. Nobody knew she played the piano but when she built the big house she bought a big organ. There is a story that as a young girl she played the piano at the church. There was another young girl who wanted to be the "Piano Player." One Sunday the piano stool was missing. That girl had hidden it.

Gilreath Manor had a large patio with a six-foot tall, curved brick wall with planters and this is where she entertained. She loved to entertain and usually had two hundred to three hundred people at each party. She hosted several fund raisers for the Cancer Society with a guest list of 1500 and tickets were $20 per person. In 1977 the party was on her seventy-fifth birthday on July fourth. Guests parked at the bottom of the hill, so, she had a big wooden wagon built to transport guest from the bottom of the hill to the house. The wagon was painted red with red plaid cushions and seating for twenty riders. The wagon also proudly displayed two flags: one American and one Tennessean. The wagon was pulled by the tractor, which was also red.

She had never traveled until later in life when she and Roy went to Santo Domingo in the Dominican Republic in March of 1971. Later that year, in August, they traveled to Holland, Switzerland, Italy and England. In London they visited with Doctors Ross and Sizzy Dougal. Sizzy is Ed Smith's sister. In 1972 she traveled, with four women friends, to Spain and Africa. In Spain they watched bull fights and spent Holy Week in Seville. From Seville they took a Mediterranean Cruise to Algiers where they rode camels and watched snake charmers.

Helma's was sold in 1988 to the Natour family (this is the same family that later opened Pete's on Union Avenue) and she stayed on one year to oversee the transition from worker to retirement. In retirement she always had a garden and sold tomatoes to the local grocery store. She was so proud of the money she earned from the tomato sales that she kept the money in a cigar box on top of the refrigerator and always told us about this week's earnings.

She was generous to a fault, not just with resources but with care and concern. If there was a scintilla of good, she would not only find it but use it to make an unfortunate situation better. When she died in 1993, we found charge sheets, from the grocery store, that had never been paid. She told us that men would come in after work for food for their families and she could not tell them no. She never tried to collect.

Some see the sign as a place to remember and others to wonder what it was, but surely it must represent something or someone special. Some remember it as a special place because they became engaged over supper or had special days at the Sunday buffet others because of monthly meetings and Helma lending anything the school needed, if she had it. The Carter High School Junior Class Play needed to borrow the small wooden picnic table that sat in the garden behind the large back porch for a scene in the play. The script called for Charlotte Cates to jump up on the table and yell something. She jumped, the table broke and she yelled, "Oh! Shit!" Folks, this happened in the Spring of 1957. Everybody who was there and still alive remembers the night that Charlotte yelled, "Oh! Shit!" Or the night that Helma's table broke.

1957 Carter High Junior Play:
Charlotte is the one with the Sword.

I probably should not tell this, but I will anyway. My brother, Doug, will laugh and my sister, Jean, will be embarrassed. The week following our mother's death, Doug stayed to help Jean and me. Our mother had her papers organized in a four-drawer filing cabinet. The three of us were seated at the kitchen table going through her papers when Doug burst-out laughing. He was laughing so hard he could not speak and just handed me the paper he had just read. I read it and joined him in laughing but when I handed it to Jean, she did not think it was funny and said, "we cannot tell anyone."

Doug said, "like hell we cannot tell, I live in Baltimore."

The paper Doug had read was her birth certificate. She was born on July fifth not July fourth as she had told all of us our whole lives. Remember all the parties celebrating her birthday on July fourth? I know she is looking down this very minute thinking, "It is okay to talk about it. It has been twenty-five years. What took you so long?"

She saw people for who they were and that is how she taught us, by her actions not her words. Food brings people together; Helma added the secret sauce of happiness in serving and being with others whether it was her family, her customers or someone who needed her help. I am amazed at what an exceptional human she was. I shared her life but did not recognize her gift until she was gone. She would be horrified at today's world but be accepting of today's people. Courage is fostered by necessity from 1908-1993 she proved that more than once. In every city, town, village, and community, there is that one special place where people congregate. They come after church and meet for lunch; the Kiwanis meet there on Wednesday, the Senior Prom is held downstairs, and sweethearts sit in a booth and share a malt. In the Carter Community that special place was always.........HELMA'S.

Paralympic Games, Atlanta (1996)

Paralympic Games, Atlanta, 1996

Working the Paralympic Games in Atlanta, Georgia in 1996 as a Track and field official remains the highlight of my life. Never before or since have I experienced so many emotions and learned so much in such a short period of time.

The Paralympic Games were held August sixteenth to the twenty-fifth, 1996. I was a Track and Field Official working Throws. The Para Games consisted of 508 events and eleven venues. A total of one-hundred nations were represented at the 1996 games and the combined total of athletes was about 3,260. The mascot was BLAZE. BLAZE is a phoenix, a mythical bird that rises from ashes to experience a renewed life. The phoenix has long been the symbol of Atlanta's rebirth after its devastation in the American Civil War, Most importantly, it is the personal personification of the will, perseverance and determination of youth and adults with physical disability to achieve full and productive lives.

The Atlanta Olympics was held July nineteenth through August fourth, 1996. The Para Games began on August sixteenth and used the same facilities and venues as the Olympics. The officials and athletes were housed in the dorms at Georgia Tech. Track and Field events were held in the new Braves Stadium while the Braves played next door in the old stadium. Throws is a field event which includes Shot, Discus, Javelin and Hammer. Officials work all practice, warm up and competitions. Meals were served in a big, white tent. Officials, coaches and athletes shared the eating facility. We were transported to the venue on buses. Only officials and athletes were allowed on the buses…. No Coaches. We wore uniforms and credentials and carried our special chairs with the Paralympic Logo on the chair back.

One morning we were traveling south on I-75 toward the Brave's Stadium when our bus and two other buses stopped in the middle of traffic because a coach had sneaked on the bus. (they thought he might be a terrorist). We had large, photo credentials which we wore around our neck and were carefully checked before being allowed inside the venue. Once inside we went to meetings, got work assignments and instruction for the day. We then walked single file out and onto the field, our chairs carried in our left hand. (After all, the Olympics had nothing on us in style and execution of an entrance.)

The Official's Motto is: Fair and Equal Treatment for All. During warm-ups athletes were standing on both side of the runway. All officials are seated and silent except for the Flight Co-Ordinator who may move around. I was the Flight Co-Ordinator for Men's Javelin and could move around to assist athletes and I noticed that two men were in a spirited discussion. One man was not even in uniform but had on jeans and a madras shirt. Big No-No. I went over to find out who they were and what was going on when Mr. Madras turned around and I saw his big, black credential. Black meant All Access, which meant I went back to officiating. I later found out he was FBI and was speaking with either the Israeli or Palestinian's Security Officer. Here we were, the Israelites on one side of the runway and the Palestinians on the other. They both had javelins.

After competition was over, we were taken back to Georgia Tech. We could always tell if there had been a bomb scare because security usually looked at our credentials and waved us through the metal protector but if there was an active bomb scare, they would pull everything out of every backpack, and this took forever but everybody accepted it in good humor. We grown-ups would bring wine in water bottles in our backpacks into the compound. We were adults, and a little libation after a twelve-to-eighteen-hour day was acceptable...to us anyway.

One day I had been officiating running events and we should have been finished by 10:00 p.m. but a storm hit. The rain was pouring, and the wind was blowing markers and chairs down the track. In Track and Field, like other sports, there is a lightning strike policy. If lighting strikes within a prescribed area, competition is stopped, and everybody must leave the track.

Competition is halted until there has been thirty minutes without a strike. I have been a certified official for forty years and have sat in rain delays that last one-two hours and ready to resume competition and another strike hit… start a new thirty minutes. Well, anyway, this day in Atlanta we got off the track at 2:30 a.m. No buses, no Marta, and no way back to Georgia Tech. We were in a part of Atlanta that has all windows and doors covered with bars. The Braves were playing next door and were hit with the same storm, and they had to sit and wait to finish the ball game. The ball game was over about the same time as the track meet, so we were all leaving at the same time. In the parking lot I spied a car with Chattanooga license plates. Headed toward the car was a man, a woman and two children. I walked up to them and showed them my credentials and asked if they were driving up I-75 and would they give us a ride to the Georgia Tech exit? They took us all the way to our gate. There were two men officials with me, and they could not believe I would walk up to a total stranger and ask for a ride… And they were more surprised when the man said yes. We bought souvenirs and sent to the two children as a thank you. The two officials, one from New York and the other from the Mid-West, told everybody, "Stay close to Patti and you will never have to walk home."

One of my favorite memories is of a late-night ride in the Golf Cart Train inside the compound. I was by myself and sitting behind me were three teenage boys and I have no idea who they were, where they were from or their sport. What I hope I will never forget is their laughter. One would say something and all three would kill themselves laughing, somebody else would say something and there would be another big burst of laughter. I have been to Russia, Africa, Europe and East Tennessee and have no idea what language they were speaking. All three were blind.

We worked long hours in the sun, rain and any element Atlanta could muster in August. We worked long hours, with little free time or sleep. The track event that was over at 2:30 a.m. was followed by breakfast in the tent at 6:00 a.m.

Working the Para Games was and is the highlight of my life. I am so grateful to have had that most wonderful experience.

You Cannot Do That!

One nice summer Saturday afternoon in the late 1970s a man drove up in a pickup truck to my farm. I had never seen him or his truck before. He was from the Amoco Oil Company and was informing me that on Monday they were going to begin testing for gas and oil... he explained that they would be blowing holes, in a straight line, all across my property. After he had explained this to me, I explained to him, "No You Will Not." He explained again, that yes, they would because they owned the Mineral Rights, which we called Underground Rights, and includes anything underneath the ground's surface. The Underground Rights for all the properties had been sold forty to fifty years ago and the current owners understood this. In my case what he didn't understand was that I owned a twenty-acre Surface Reservation. This reservation meant that he could not cross the twenty-acres nor touch one blade of grass.

From my property he went next door to Doug's farm. On Monday the oil company came in began blowing holes all across Doug's property. When they completed the testing, they left holes and wire and other debris across Doug's farm. He had cows in the field and the holes and wires were a hazard to the cows. About two weeks after they left Doug's well caved in.

At that time if a company damaged your property the company would decide damages and it was a "take it or leave it" deal. The property owner had no choice but to take what was offered or take nothing. After Doug realized his well

37

was ruined and his field was damaged, I asked him what he was going to do, and he said he had no idea. What we did decide was to find out if there were other property owners who had been contacted by the Oil Company. We were surprised to find that there were several owners who had been approached… So…we decided to call a meeting.

We met in the banquet room of Helma's. The first meeting we had about twenty people show up. Anybody who wished to speak was asked to state their name and address. Over against the wall was a big man dressed in bibbed overalls and a black tee shirt. He also had a big black beard and sat with his arms crossed over his chest. He hadn't said anything and finally somebody asked who he was, and he did not want to say. But after being pushed he said he was from "near Chattanooga" which is one-hundred miles from us. The light dawned…he was a Ringer, and this was the first inkling that we were on to something.

We formed a group called The Concerned Property Owners. I was elected President (probably because my mother owned the restaurant where we were meeting). The Oil Company found out that we had formed a group, and we were just beginning to find out how all of this worked. For instance, if a farmer had a corn crop, the oil company, could just plow right through the crop to get where they wanted to drill. Also, at the drill site they built big saline sludge ponds and other debris. As I mentioned earlier, we all knew we did not own the underground rights but did not understand what all it meant. I understood what Surface Rights meant.

The oil company contacted me about setting up a meeting with their engineers to discuss their plans. They told me that they would only meet with me and two other people. I explained that all our group would be invited to the meeting. Then they said that they would not meet in the banquet room but only in the library at the elementary school. (The banquet room could hold two-hundred people, but the library could hold twenty to thirty people.) So, we met at the library.

We looked, for the most part, like the Bumpkins they thought we were and there they were fancy engineers from Atlanta and New Orleans. My, my, they brought massive, full-color maps that mapped everything. They talked, showed maps, charts, photographs and data for all kinds of things. Bottomline, we just wanted to know is what and when are you will begin and what can we expect. After the big meeting with the engineers …. Oh! and I forgot to mention that all three of the engineers were here for two days and stayed at the Hyatt. We thought that was "pretty tall cotton" and also, we knew we had somebody's attention. After the meeting we decided we needed to hire a lawyer. We had no money so one of the farmers took off his John Deere cap and passed it around and each of us gave what we could. That is how we raised the money. Incidentally the farmer with the cap is the same man, when we found out there was talk of trouble, who asked if I would like for him to come sit in one of the trees in my front yard with his shotgun.

We decided to just be watchful. We hired the only lawyer who would speak with us, David Buuck from Knoxville. David took our case all the way to the Tennessee Supreme Court. Doug had done research on the definition of oil and gas. The Squirrels were all the same things. We lost the case to keep the company off our land, but we did manage to get two pieces of legislation passed. One- The Company may not come through a crop until the crop is harvested, and Two- The property owner would have the right to go to arbitration to determine damages.

As far as I know, the oil company never did any drilling in our area. What I did learn was that We, Us, Farmers and Neighbors, came together to say, "You Cannot Do That."

Rock Trucks: County Chronicle Reports on Rock Trucks (1986)

Fancy Meadow Farm, Strawberry Plains, TN

In 1986, we lived in Strawberry Plains in Jefferson County. A four-lane highway was two blocks from our house. Everyone in the area knew the sight and sounds of the Rock Trucks ---huge dump trucks that hauled rock from a nearby quarry. The drivers would race each other up the four lanes, drinking beer, high up in the cab with a load of fifteen tons of rock and gravel. A few months before, a loaded truck was traveling east on Asheville Highway when the driver lost the brakes and crashed into several vehicles parked at a strip mall. My boys learned that their job was to look for the Rock Trucks before we pulled onto the highway.

One afternoon a school bus stopped to let a six-year-old girl off in front of her home. A Rock Truck passed between the school bus and the ditch, hitting and killing the little girl instantly. The brakes on the huge truck had failed, again!

I had given up my teaching job and opened a sign shop in East Knoxville. I also owned the County Chronicle, a monthly newspaper that covered all the communities in East Knox County, Strawberry Plains in Jefferson County and Holston Hills in East Knoxville. I was at work when an old friend called. We were discussing the tragedy of losing the little girl when he said, "You own a Newspaper, do something." I asked him what he thought I could do, and he said, "my cousin, Keith Bissell, is in Nashville and is head of the Transportation Department for Tennessee." I called Keith, he said he would send me contact information for the Transportation Chief in East Tennessee located in Kingsport. The chief came down to Knoxville, and I drove him around the truck routes. This is when I found out that the drivers would take side roads to avoid being stopped for inspection by the Department of Transportation Officers. If there were violations the truck would be parked until all repairs or violations were remedied and inspected. A parked truck earns no money. The drivers were paid by the load so that explains the speeding, racing and general disregard for highway safety.

A few months before the little girl was killed, a loaded truck was traveling east on Asheville Highway, lost his brakes and crashed into to several vehicles parked at a small strip mall. This crash, coming so close to the death of the six-year-old, made investigation mandatory. I was assured by the Chief that all these infractions were being investigated and would begin inspections. I got a call from an officer out of the Kingsport Office asking if I would meet with him and one other officer. He asked that our conversation and meeting be kept confidential. We met at a restaurant, where they told me that the reason that so many incidents of accidents and near accidents were ignored was because the Chief "was on the take." I reported all of this to Keith in Nashville. He had initiated surprise inspections, and my job was to alert the media. Up to this point, nothing much had been found in the way of violations. After Keith found out about the Chief tipping off the trucking company, he planned a massive, middle-of-the-night inspection of all the trucks in the fleet. I was invited to these inspections in the past but thought I would be more valuable just to lay low and keep my eyes and ears open. Also, it had already been suggested that I might want to be more vigilant when driving alone or at night. To be very plain, I was more than a little scared, but after the big, surprise, middle-of-the-night inspection, most of the fleet was grounded. I cannot remember, but I think fines were levied against the company.

About two years later, I was at work when a distraught woman called and said, "are you that woman who owns the newspaper?" She then told me that the school bus stopped in front of her house to let her children off and a Rock Truck came flying by between her and the bus. Until the truck passed, she did not know if her children were alive or dead. They were fined and the incident was reported to Tennessee Department of Transportation. Once again, the County Chronicle had a Rock Truck story. The paper was a monthly so the closest we could come to a scoop was a week...I loved that little paper.

Unleafed

It is the eighteenth day of Spring in Knoxville and seeds sprouting, bulbs blossoming and tree's leafing. This is normally a time of renewal and optimism but then there was last Tuesday, the eighteenth day of Spring. I am retired so usually the weeks are not so busy, but this week was the exception. Amazon notified me of unusual activity on my account. Somebody had bought a Nintendo and four gift cards. The credit card company from the bank notified me that somebody had bought a $799 phone on my account. Both companies removed the charges and sent new cards.

I had spent the last two weeks trying to decide whether or not to buy a 2005, forty-two ft Motor Home from a longtime friend. My friend was living in the RV in Fort Myers, Florida but wanted to move into a condo. I have two sons who were less than enthusiastic about me driving a forty-two ft, bus-sized vehicle, but on Wednesday they said they would drive it to Houston for me. I decided to buy this most wonderfully beautiful RV. Both boys were in the process of buying homes in Houston: Adam from Salt Lake City and Solon from Henderson, North Carolina. They both have jobs and wives but decided they could fly to Fort Myers and drive the RV to Houston, Adam from Salt Lake and Solon from Houston. My job was to decide to sell my RV; register, get new tags and insurance for the new RV, and rent a space in an RV Park in Houston where the boys would leave it on Saturday. My friend, the seller, said that the RV was registered in Montana because Montana has no sales

44

tax. Tennessee has a nine percent sales tax, with a few add-ons, making it the highest in the country

I began the third Wednesday of Spring with a doctor's appointment to check my eyelid surgery and to look into storage unit for my track gear. I am a USATF certified master's official and our uniform is a shirt provided by Meet Management, khaki skirt, shorts or pants and white running shoes of which I have five pairs. I had packed all this along with my backpack in a plastic container. I never found it so I bought a new pair of shorts and wore hiking boots because it was raining. The Tennessee Relays is a three - day meet held at the University of Tennessee, Knoxville beginning on Thursday and I had to check-in by 9:00 a.m. for Covid test.

Petie, my one-year-old Jack Russell, had vomited three times during the night and had an intestinal irritation and was expelling blood. I took her to the Vet and was told she might need surgery Thursday night because they did not know if there was an infection or obstruction. Infection is treatable but obstruction would require surgery.

I made it to the track by 9:00 a.m. and reported to the Long Jump Pit. It poured rain all day. Track meets, like other outdoor events, are halted only for lightning. There was no lightning, so we continued in the rain, all day.

I picked up Petie and was told to take her home, along with three medications, because they were not for certain she had an obstruction but to call Friday morning.

The boys sent flight schedules. On Friday, they arrived in Fort Myers at 4:30 p.m. and took an Uber to the RV Park to get the new RV. I was at the track on a glorious, bright, sunny day. Big storms were predicted for Saturday, so meet management moved all Saturday events to Friday. While I was at the track, the boys checked out the RV. Adam has a CDL license, so Adam was the driver. He was to drive it to Houston where I had rented a site in an RV park in North West Houston. Solon called me at the track to say the top speed of the RV was twenty-five mph. They said, "Mom, it will not run." The boys made the decision to return the RV to the RV Park, park it and leave the key. Now they are on foot, no hotel and no return flight to Houston. They walked to the Holiday Inn and a couple was having "Date Night" and wanted a room. There were no rooms, but the couple invited the boys to ride with them to find a room. They drove for one hour before they found a hotel with one room available, and the couple, who lived in Fort Myers, said they would just go home and let the boys have the room. They booked flights to Houston for Saturday.

On the fourth Saturday of spring, I had to figure how to undo the RV Sale, undo the LLC in Montana, undo the insurance, cancel sale site for my RV, and cancel the one-month reservation at RV park in Houston.

The vet's office closed at 4:00 p.m. on Friday but they left food for Petie at the pizza place next door. I was at the track until 9:00 p.m. and was too tired to pick the food up on Friday night.

Saturday, Petie and I were driving to pick up her food. It was raining but I noticed the trees. They looked so fresh, leafed out and beautiful. Then I saw a lone tree with no leaves...unleafed... and that is exactly how I felt...unleafed.

Home Is Where You Park It!

Patti's First RV

"Home Sweet Home: where u can scratch where it itches...even if it is in your britches." ~Helma

February 2017, 7:00 p.m., I had pain in my upper left chest that would not go away. I walked, stretched, twisted but nothing would relieve the pain, so, I called my neighbor, Susi. I said, "Susi, I think I am having a heart attack will you take me to the hospital?" She was scared half to death, but she took me and stayed for a while. They kept me, ran multiple tests and all this time I was hooked up to several machines. That night I was seventy-seven years old, lying in an emergency room cubical, cold (the temperature was almost above freezing) and scared. Those hours allowed for lots of thinking. One thing I thought about was all the things I always wanted to do but never had. The one I remember the most is, I always wanted an RV. I had never known anybody who had one, never been in one but just always thought I would love to have one. I got home from the hospital at 2:00 a.m. and went to work at 9:00 a.m. The hunt was on!

My library of Recreational Vehicle Information was a big round zero. I learned this immediately. There are five classes of recreational vehicles. Class A, class B, Class C, Fifth Wheel and Travel Trailers. Classes A, B and C are Motor Homes, and you drive your home. Fifth Wheel and Travel Trailers must be pulled by a big truck. I also found out that RV's can be very expensive--- up to over one million dollars expensive. At age seventy-seven, I was looking for something less obvious, grandiose? I had known for a long time that "being able to pay for something was not the same as being able to afford it." I fell in love with the first RV I saw, a brand-new Mercedes Class B Van—priced at one-hundred and fifty-thousand. I had no idea you could spent so much money on a van. It was nice but *one hundred and fifty thousand dollars*? Now that my feet had been attached to the ground of reality…onward!

I bought a 2005 used Class C motor home which was ugly. I stripped the graphics, installed new graphics on all four exterior walls, bought new tires, new roof and painted the interior. There is something about RV interiors that brings out the worst in designers…. ugly…. double ugly and triple ugly. Unless it was fabric it got painted.

Patti works on her RV, 2021.

Up to this point my boys did not know about the new acquisition. I did not tell them because I did not want to hear, "Mom, that is too dangerous, you cannot drive a twenty-five-foot vehicle, and what if something happens to you?" After I bought it, I learned I could drive it and told the boys it is not your money or responsibility. I bought insurance. After the "Rollie Home," as I called it was roadworthy, dog and I took our first road trip, thirty miles up I-40 to an RV Camp on the river. I was introduced to discrimination in the RV World. Only Class A rigs could park by the river. The rest of us had to park on the back row away from the river. In fact, there are Class A only RV Parks where my Class C Rollie Home is not welcome under any circumstances. Discrimination was alive and well in the RV World. The learning curve for me was steep – how to hook up water and sewer, un-hook and store equipment, chemical treatment for water and sewage holding tanks, and how to care for and operate a generator. When a semi-truck passes on the interstate the RV is pushed to the right the driver must not overcorrect, you also must swing wide when turning so that the back end of the rig does not hit the gas pump or other object. Also, it is extremely important to lock all outside storage compartments so items do not blow out during travel. Experience is an excellent teacher.

The first real road trip was from Knoxville, Tennessee, to Key West, Florida, to surprise my brother on his seventy-fifth birthday. Two-thousand miles round trip. The drive was a wonderful learning adventure. For instance, the people of Miami are not nice, they are assholes in fact. I needed to change lanes, but nobody would let me over, so dog, rig, and I wound up downtown at lunch hour. I just kept turning left until I found I-95 south. Also, I learned that if I missed an exit, to just stay cool and composed, get off at the next exit and turn around. This is why time management is so important. Leave early so there is enough time for "screw-up time." I do not like to drive in the dark – either morning or night. Just be "at the gate like a Bronco ready to ride at first light" is usually my plan.

Doug and Patti, Key West, 2021

Gas is expensive and I read if you want to save money in an RV, do not drive. Do I fill up when the tank is half empty? half full? Do not panic until you only have a quarter of a tank and not a gas station in sight. Always park with a full tank of gas because, in an emergency, the generator can run electricity for water, heat and lights. Propane runs hot water, heater, and stove. The generator runs off gas.

My brother, Doug, has a house in Key West but no place to park the RV, so the dog and I stayed in an RV Park on Stock Island, next to Key West. He has been going to Key West for twenty-five years and has lots of long-time friends. The village folk and chickens are all interesting – more than most places. Doug and his wife Joy are busy, active, fun folk. Always something or somebody to see or sit with over good food and a beverage…lots of beverages. One morning Joy was busy, so Doug and I had breakfast in town. We had biscuits and gravy and wine- now that was different – good, but different.

My first trip was uneventful in that there were no mishaps. A hurricane had hit in August and there were marks of destruction all along the Keys. Irma hit in August followed by Maria two weeks later. Travel home was incident free. Feeling Emboldened!

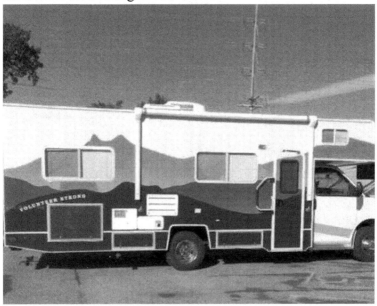

Patti's RV

I Wonder

I like people and I like to drive. One day in 2015 I saw an advertisement looking for drivers for a service called Uber and wondered if I could do that. I applied, was accepted and started driving. Uber is a taxi-like service with the difference of fares being booked and paid online. The company takes a share of each fare. This was a totally new experience for me. I knew how to drive but I had to learn to accept rides from the app on my phone. Our workweek ended at 4:00 a.m. on Monday and by Tuesday our earnings were posted and deposited in our bank account by Thursday. We were told to not expect tips, but if offered we may accept. There was no pay for waiting or cancellation. These policies have changed, after waiting two minutes the rider is automatically charged. Once a reservation is made the rider has five minutes to cancel and after five minutes the rider is charged a cancellation fee. One time I was asked to wait while a rider changed hotel rooms and another time while a man ate his cereal. If you like people and driving, Uber is a good part-time job. I live in the middle of downtown where there are hotels, restaurants, hospitals and six blocks from the University of Tennessee.

I have two boys, Adam in Utah and Solon in North Carolina, and I did not tell them until I had been driving for two weeks. First, I did not know if I would be able to figure all this out or learn how all this worked, so I did not want to say anything until I was sure I could drive. Finally, I told

Solon and he said, "Mom are you that desperate for money?"
I said, "no, but a girl can always use a little extra."

There are three kinds of riders: Workers, Lookers, and
Talkers. The Worker gets into the car and immediately gets
on the phone or laptop or both; the Looker just rides and
looks; the Talker will talk about any subject.

The Talker is my favorite because I like to talk; I like to
find out where they are from, why they are here, how long
they will stay and if they need help finding anything. It did
not take long for me to learn to respect each rider. Most of
my trips are short but I have and will take longer ones. I
remember two long trips: one to Pilgrim, Tennessee, and the
other to Asheville, North Carolina. I picked up a large,
grumpy man from the bus station. I asked him for a
destination, and he mumbled, I asked again and finally
understood that he was saying Pilgrim. I had never in my life
heard of Pilgrim and when asked where it was, he mumbled
again. Finally, I put it on GPS and found it was north, almost
into Kentucky, over an hour's drive from Knoxville.

By this time, I am a little scared but drive on. After a
while he told me his story. He was from Detroit and had been
on the bus overnight and was tired. He had a friend who
asked him to take him by work so he could get his paycheck
and then to the bank to cash the check. My rider said he
stopped in a convenience store and when he came out his
friend had stolen his car. The friend was apprehended and
was being held in Pilgrim, Tennessee, and the car was being
held for pick-up by owner. Now I understood why he
mumbled. He had been taken advantage of by his so-called
friend, and had been on a bus overnight. The other long-

distance fare was to Asheville and came from the bus station. The bus company has screwed up two fares, and these two men were going to have a twenty-four-hour layover. The bus company paid their Uber fee to Asheville.

I have been scared once and angry once. I arrived to pick up a young woman at a hotel and she asked if I would wait while she changed rooms. After a fifteen-minute wait, she got into the car but would not give me her destination and said she would give me directions. My mistake. The first stop was as at an old rundown house next to a junk yard. She went around to the back of the house and returned in a couple of minutes. The second stop was in the projects where this large woman, whose eyes were swimming in her head, got into the car. The third stop was to a small house in a bad neighborhood across the river. The project woman went into the house while the first woman walked up and down the street smoking.

This is when it dawned on me, I might be in a bit of trouble. Here I am in a 2012 navy blue Sentra with no identification, looking for all the world like a "wheelman for a Drug Deal." I returned to the projects and then the hotel where I was offered and accepted a thirty-dollar tip. After leaving the hotel I drove straight to the police station where I handed my license to an officer and explained what I had just done. He explained that if we had been under surveillance and had been stopped, I would have been arrested but not charged after Uber verified my information.

The angry time was when I arrived at a pick-up address only to discover that the rider lived in the middle of the bridge, according to the address she had given. I called her and she said she was at Market Square. Did I know where that was? My condo is one and a half blocks from Market Square, and I have lived there since 1993 – so- yes, I know where Market Square is. She got into the passenger seat and I asked for a destination and she said her boyfriend would tell me. I had learned to not begin a trip without a destination. The boyfriend was at the other end of the block waiting to be picked up and when he got into the back seat I asked for a destination and he simply got out of the car, and never said a word. She began screaming at him right across my face. This is when I asked her to get out of the car, which she did not want to do. So, I told her, "You cannot ride in this car." I never did check to see how many stars she gave me.

I like people and I like driving, so I enjoy earning a little money in such a pleasant way. The Talkers are interesting and driving gives me a reason to get outside. "I wonder" got me started but never giving up because I made some dumb mistakes like turning off directions, not following directions, and talking too much at the beginning kept me going.

Da Pins

In 2023, I was living in Spring, Texas, and shopped at CVS. It was a big store and I never had trouble finding items...except this one time. I was looking for Depends, an underwear for women. I knew they must have them but could not find them, so I asked (in a small voice) a young female employee: "Where are the Depends?" She had absolutely no idea so she said she would look on her phone. I stood as she searched her phone. Finally, she showed me a picture and asked, "Is this what you are looking for?" She showed me a picture of Safety Pins.————

Da Pins

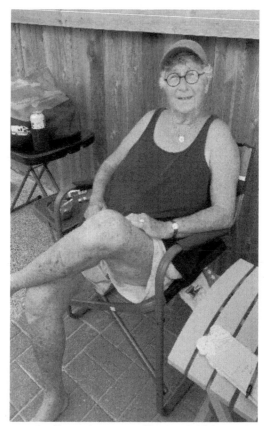

Port Aransas, Texas, 2020

Downtown

The 100 Block of Gay Street

Information from The History Project of Gay Street by Jack Neely

In 1850s Gay Street was a muddy track but was first paved in 1854 and was recognized as one of the nation's great streets by the American Planning Association. In 1883 the street witnessed a bloody a three-way gun fight between Thomas O'Conner and General Joseph Mabry. The street was raised in 1919 to meet the viaduct over the railroad tracks and covered the basements of the buildings in the 100 Block, which became known as "Underground Knoxville" in the 1970's. In the 1920's meetings were held to form a new National Park, the Great Smoky Mountains.

Life on Gay Street

In the 1990s the 100 Block of Gay Street was an exciting place to live. It was the beginning of life again in the boarded up, broken windows, rundown and empty buildings block. Jo and Jimmy Mason were the first to discover, buy and renovate the building at 124 S. Gay in the Commerce Building. They were the first residents of the new 100 Block. They were the pioneers in bringing life back to downtown, which they did with no tax incentives but with their vision and their money. They first bought the building at 124 S. Gay, then later bought the Rebori building on the corner of Gay and Summit Hill. This building became the show place of downtown and everybody wanted to have parties and events there. The Masons allowed parties to help introduce the 100 Block and downtown to the rest of the area.

Commerce Building

In 1993 I bought one half of the fifth floor in the 120 Commerce Building, unit 501. There were three residential floors below street level, the fourth floor, now street level, for retail or business offices and the fifth, sixth and seventh were residential. Originally all residential floors were divided into front units facing Gay Street and the back units facing the alley. Unit 501 faced the street and was one floor above the street. It was dirty with rusted conduit hanging down, rotted boards and the floor was so dirty you couldn't tell if it was concrete or wood. I built a 1,145-square-foot condo. In the early days I would be the only person in the building at night. There were two businesses in the building, but neither were open at night. I only got frightened one night. I was sitting up in bed reading and this feeling of absolute fear came over me. I understood that I was safe, doors locked, one floor above the street so nobody could get in, but I am convinced that there was somebody in the building who should not have been there.

Patti's Condo on 120 S Gay St.

In 1994 David Dewhirst was looking at the building on the west side of the 100 Block at 133 S. Gay Street when Jimmy Mason walked up and said, "young man you should buy this building," so he did. I lived directly across the street from 133 and I watched as he rebuilt the building. It was amazing because a boat appeared in the living room. The boat actually housed the bathroom which was certainly different. So was David. He was soooo georgeous… still is. After he moved in, I went over to welcome him to the block. He had built a deck on the back of the unit and had a hammock on a frame, but the hammock part was laying on the deck. I said" David, don't you think that is a little close to the deck?" And he said, "I had women in there with me." He also had a big TV on the north wall in the living room, which I could see because there was no window treatment. I used to watch his TV and it was always interesting. 133 S. Gay was his first downtown building but not his last. He now owns about half of downtown Knoxville.

Hung outside Patti's Door at Her Condo, 120 S Gay St.

The Homeless on Gay Street

Knoxville Area Rescue Ministries, or K.A.R.M., opened in 1960, a local mission that was housed in our block for the first ten years I lived there. During the day the homeless took up all the sidewalks around the northwest corner of Gay Street and Jackson Avenue. The homeless did pretty much as they pleased. They had sex, sold and bought drugs, and slept in our doorways. The mission was directly across from the Arts Alliance in the Emporium and there was one old woman who would wait until somebody would exit the Emporium and flash them. Lisa Zenni, the director at the

63

Alliance, said, "the women that were flashed were incensed and said they would not be back, but the men would say, 'see you next week'."

In my opinion, there are three kinds of Homeless or Street People: people down on their luck who just need a hand up to get their lives back on track, the alcoholic, drug addicted or the mentally ill, and those who choose the homeless lifestyle. Then there are the Regulars… the ones always asking for money and keep telling the same story, week-in and week-out. The young women who ask for money to buy formula for their baby and you try telling them about the mission and where they can get whatever they need but they do not listen and are halfway down the block before you finish a sentence. Help is not what they want, money is what they want. Some are pretty clever… one young man would carry a one-gallon empty gas can up and down the street where the bars have outside tables and ask for gas money. My favorite was a middle-aged woman who always said she need money to visit her mother in Nashville. One Friday night Bobby George and I had worked late at the sign shop and we were going to get a beer at Market Square. We had parked at the corner of Union and Walnut when she came up and asked for money to go see her, old sick mama in Nashville. I said, "You mean to tell me that old woman is not dead yet." Bobby's eyes got about as big as saucers and the woman took off. She did not remember that this was the third time in two weeks she had asked me the same thing.

Somebody Sleeping on a Bench on the 100 Block of Gay St.

One young man would tell us that he was an engineer at Sea-Ray, at the forks-of-the-river and needed gas money to get to work. These were our neighbors who lived across the street. We learned to live together.

Some chose to not live at the Mission and Rodney was one. He and I shared the same birthday. One year he had four empty cigar boxes, and he let me choose one for my birthday present. I still have it. He would pester Jo Mason about pulling weeds along the side of her building. She would finally give in and give him $20. He would pull three weeds and be gone.

My sign shop was down on Jackson Avenue in the Old City and there was this interesting street person... I cannot remember his name but he was there every day and some days he would stop and have a sensible conversation and others he would be off the wall. One hot summer day he was walking east on Jackson wearing cowboy boots and Bermuda shorts. He had spray painted the boots with green spray paint while wearing them because he had also painted his legs. Another time he just walked up and down the street wearing a metal tube (conduit) attached to a shower head around his neck. I found out that when he was taking his medication, he was fine but off his meds he was bizarre. I was told he was taken to Oak Ridge and Oak Ridge brought him back to the Knox County Line and put him out on Pellissippi Parkway where he was hit and killed by a hit-and-run driver. A donation was taken in our neighborhood to help with his burial.

Trapper was another of my favorites. When he needed money, he would stop by the shop to see if I had any work for him. He could fix almost anything; he was always clean and well dressed. The church ladies loved him because he would help them set up and take down their tents at the corner of Broadway and Fifth Avenue on Saturday morning. As payment they would give him matching sets of shorts and shirts. Sometimes, after he worked for me, he would go to work at an automotive paint shop. I paid him in cash as did the paint business. One day after he left the paint place, he was followed by two men who robbed and beat him so badly that he was in the hospital for over a week.

There was one really big and scary, mentally ill man, who would walk up and down the 100 Block talking to himself and waving his arms... He was obviously upset about something. I was afraid of him and if he was walking on our block, I would not park but would just drive around the block until he was gone. He had started going into the Arts Alliance space in the Emporium and Lisa Zinni, the Director, had trouble getting him to leave, but this one day, as I was going into my building, she had had it... She got him out and was charging up the sidewalk headed our way. I asked her what was going on and she told me about dealing with this man. He had just gone into my building and locked himself in the restroom on the street level. The police officers did not like dealing with these people and they told him to come out of the restroom... Silence... after a long time... he finally came out and was taken away.

Sundown in the city was a free concert on Thursday nights for twelve weeks at Market Square beginning in 1997. In 2004 the concert drew eight-thousand to ten-thousand people each night. Ashley Capps, President of A.C. Entertainment, was the creator and producer of Sundown. He said, "it is not just a concert but a community celebration." One Thursday night I was going up to Sundown and saw Bernadette, owner of Preservation Pub, standing in the street looking up at the building at the northeast corner of Market Square. She was supervising a large lift truck trying to get a drunk off the roof because he was throwing beer bottles onto the Sundown crowd. They had already sent a small lift bucket up, but the drunk was so drunk he could not stand up, so they had to send up a platform up to get the old guy down.

The Gay Street viaduct was torn down in 2005 and rebuilt. It was closed for over two years and after it was finished, we were not allowed to drive on it for several months. No explanation was ever given.

Our block got a complete makeover, all utilities were put underground, wide sidewalks, new lighting, benches, trees, parking bays and parking meters. The total block renovation began on February 23, 2009, and was completed on September 27, 2012. It began with a huge hole on the west side of the street which took several months then another huge hole was opened on the east side of the street to accommodate the new underground utilities.

The 100 Block restaurants were varied and excellent. Harold's Deli had been in business over fifty years. We gathered for breakfast or lunch, individually or in groups. Harold and Addie were dear, dear people, and so was their long-time staff. Saturday mornings we would meet for breakfast. Our group of eight to ten people would always sit in the far back tables and the eighteen to twenty Catholics, after Mass, would sit at the tables up front.

A restaurant called CRU Bistro was our Wednesday night place to be because of the-really good half priced hamburgers. There would be anywhere from eighteen to twenty of us and the drinks and conversation were always exceptional.

Our up-scale restaurant was Knox Mason. It was owned by Matt Gallaher who insisted on an interesting and changeable menu. The space was small so we usually needed reservations.

Thelma and Louise of Gay Street

In the very early days around the corner on Jackson Avenue was the Underground, a night club and an event center. It closed at 3:00 a.m. and the young people loved it because they could get stumble down drunk, and nobody cared. They made a lot of noise coming down the street and one morning they woke me up, so I just sat in the window and watched. A young man jumped and was swinging on Jo and Jimmy Mason's awning. (This was when Jo and Jimmy lived two doors from me). I yelled at the drunken gymnast to get down...and he did...then he told what I could do to myself...then he jumped back up hung and swung on the awning until he pulled it off the wall onto the street. I did not see any point in calling the Masons with the bad news in the middle of the night; the news could just wait.

After that incident I went down and just stood and watched when the club closed. There was a KPD officer there and I asked him if it did not bother him that he was allowing these young drunks to go get into cars and drive away. He told me he was just there to keep the peace.

After this Jo and I decided something needed to be done so we started video-taping the young drunks after they left the club at 3:00 a.m. Some were polite and told us they had a designated driver; some grabbed their zippers but mostly we were ignored by everybody. Nobody wanted to hear what we were trying to tell them. We tried to give the video tapes to city officials, but nobody was interested so.........we decided to check out the Boiler Room. It was underneath the Underground and opened at 3:00 a.m. and closed at 6:00 a.m.

which gave the downtown workers who got off work at 3:00 a.m. some place to go. We were too afraid to stand outside so we sat in Jo's Volvo station wagon with a child seat in the back (we thought the car seat made us look less threatening). We got hungry so we went up to Weigel's and got some munchies. Again, we were videoing, and a woman came out with two small children. That was sad but then a really big scary thing happened. Jo had the video camera in her lap when a big dude came out and was walking straight for our car. Jo was saying, "what do we do? what do we do?" I could not speak, my eyes were too big. Just as he got to Jo's door he reached out and opened his car door which was parked next to us. That was it... we were through... we had had enough drama for one night. Thelma and Louise of Gay Street went home.

The HOLA Festival was given permission to hold their festival on October 9, 2010, in the 100 Block and 200 Block of Gay Street. It was chaos and a disaster from the beginning for the residents of the 100 Block. Residents were denied entrance to their building, smoke from the cookers went into residential units and the music was so loud that nobody could hear their TV. Complaints began immediately when the residents realized how bad and how long this would be in the block. I think one resident either sued or threatened to sue because of damages. This was a bad idea from the beginning...for everybody...and never happened again...thank goodness.

Judy McCarthy, Patti, and Jo Mason

February 1, 2014, the McClung warehouse on west Jackson Avenue caught fire. The fire was scary for our block as well as the Old City because of the embers that were blowing down the street. I went across the street to alert any residents of the fire. Judy and Dennis McCarthy went down to Anne Marie Tugwell's because of the smoke. I went up on our roof and found a golfball-sized ember and was afraid to leave until I thought we were out of danger. I was told that embers blew as far as the Old City. As a neighborhood we felt as if we had dodged a bullet.

Patti and Mille visiting Judy McCarthy in Santa Fe, New Mexico

In 2022 I sold my unit after living there for twenty-seven years. I finally figured out that I was just too old to live there. I had bad knees and hips, and walking had become a problem. I love the 100 Block, downtown, and my neighborhood. Do I miss it? Certainly, I probably always will because I was a part of Camelot.

Patti and her new shotgun

Kiss and Make Up

It is hard to keep up with everything...like time left on a parking meter. There are several reasons why one overstays the time limit, but the number one reason is forgetting. In today's busy world there are a whole lot of distractions and remembering to hurry and put more money in the meter is one. Also, there is an enormous difference between residential parking and commercial parking. If you have a business meeting or need to go shopping it is easier to keep up with meter time than when you are in your home. For instance, if you are home there are any number of reasons you forget, i.e. sit down to read an article and fall asleep, talk on the phone, or decide on the spur of the moment to clean out the closet.

I don't know if this has ever happened to you but do you remember the panic you feel when you remember, "Oh, Lord I think I am out of money at the meter"? You hurry, find your shoes, find some coins (this was before the card meters), forget you coat (except when it is raining), and rush down the stairs, through the lobby and down the street to find there are still have a few minutes left, you are out of minuets but nobody has noticed, or you have a TICKET.

Twelve – fifteen years ago this happened to me. Several times I overstayed the meter time until I owed the city almost one thousand dollars. I did not do this all by myself. I had help from my grandson, Seth, who was living with me at the time. Eventually the letter arrives that says pay this amount by this date or else. This is scary and is also very serious. My

Chronicles and Narratives

buddies, Jo Mason and Diane Mack, and I decided the best course of action was Night Court. Off we three went, up the hill with a great deal of optimism that I would not be kept. Some judges are understanding and others not so much. Also, the tone of the judge's voice is an indicator of how much trouble you are in. Well, anyway, I explained to the judge that with all the construction and street rebuilding it was hard to find parking. The Gay Street Viaduct was torn down and it took over two years to rebuild and when it was finished it sat there, roped off, for about eight months. We were not allowed to park and were given no explanation.

Well, I explained and then it was the judge's turn. I did not have to pay the total amount, just court cost, and was put on a payment plan for the remainder. I always wondered what they did with my money, but at least I had been given a chance to *Kiss and Make Up*.

The Pooper Troopers

Most folk would not think that being called a Pooper Trooper is a term of accomplishment, but we did. In 1993, Gay Street, which runs through the heart of the business district for restaurants, hotels, shops and offices, was in the beginning of revitalization. There were broken and boarded up windows, homeless people sleeping in doorways, a bar here and there, and just generally, a lot of rundown areas. You could walk, buck-naked, down the middle of Gay Street after five p.m. because there was nobody to see you.

Jo and Jimmy Mason were the first to jump in with their own vision and money when they bought the building in the middle of the 100 Block on the east side of Gay Street. They brought that building back to life, even sheltering the Rachmaninoff Statue, since it was moved to the World's Fair Park. They then moved to the Rebori Building, a four- floor building, located at the south end of the 100 Block and next to the O.P. Jenkins parking lot. They turned into a Show Place. They were gracious enough to allow agencies and friends to use their home to entertain. They used all four floors. Each floor was five-thousand square feet. The first floor was Jimmy's wine cellar, where he housed hundreds of bottles. During construction, some homeless found and took 400 bottles and when they were empty, they discarded them on the sidewalks and alleys. The second floor was street level with the front of the building used as an office and the guest bedroom was in the back. I had never seen a twelve-foot shower curtain before. The third floor was the kitchen, dining and sitting areas. The kitchen was amazing. It had a twenty- foot stainless steel arch over the stove and refrigerator. The top floor was sleeping and shower space. The shower was one of the most talked about areas in the whole building because it was a twelve- foot square with two shower heads and no walls or curtains. The comment usually was "how can you stand in the middle of five thousand square feet of space with no curtains on the windows or the shower?" There was nobody to see. The main entrance to the living quarters was from the south side next to the parking lot and the offensive grassy area.

I had moved into the Commerce Building in the 100 Block in 1993. The Sterchi Building was opened in 1996 and is the tallest building in the 100 Block. One morning Jo and I were talking, and she mentioned how awful the smell was from the grassy area. Her building overlooked the grassy area where all the dogs relieved themselves. Dog owners were not picking up and as the summer temperature rose so did the stench. That morning, we decided we would put a small colored flag at each deposit of dog-doo. The first day we placed red flags, second- blue, third-yellow, and the fourth-green. By the time we had flagged all the deposits we had placed over five-hundred flags in the first week. That is a lot of flags. Since this was city-owned property, it did not take long for somebody to notice and notice they did. The newspapers, TV Stations and authorities noticed. What we found out during all the attention we were given was that there was no City Ordinance that demanded waste to be picked up by owner. This is when Robin Wilhoite from channel ten dubbed us the Pooper Troopers. Jo and I had no idea how to get a City Ordinance passed but we learned. For City Council to pass an ordinance it must have two readings. The first reading is the introduction, read and accepted, but the second reading is critical because this is when the vote is taken.

While we were dealing with the city, we were asking the property owners to put up notes in the elevators that said, "Please pickup after your pet." Everybody was cooperative except the owner of the Sterchi, and he refused to allow notes in the elevators.

My favorite Sterchi story is about a young man's aunt who was coming to visit him in his Sterchi apartment. She had recently had knee surgery and on the way to the apartment, in the hall, she stepped in dog-doo and fell on to the concrete floor. He moved shortly thereafter.

It was time for the second reading of the Pickup After Your Dog Ordinance. One of us needed to speak to council in defense of the ordinance. Jo is small and is a very calm, soft-spoken, gentle person. I told Jo, "You have got to do this because what you are I am not." The mayor thought the whole thing was funny and when he was reading the agenda he said, "maybe we should ask the young to leave the room because we have a nasty subject to discuss. Ha! Ha! Ha!" (Ha! Ha! Hell!) Jo did a great job of explaining to the council that we must be the only city in this hemisphere that does not have a pickup-after-your-pet ordinance. Knox County has one but not the City of Knoxville. The ordinance passed and a $50 fine was attached. We had won the battle but not the war.

The City Fathers top-to-bottom still made fun of us, the Pooper Troopers. I was in the first meeting of the Knoxville Police Department Hospitality Group with the Police Chief at Police Headquarters. During the introduction of services that KPD offers to residents the chief brought up the ordinance and said, "can you imagine we are on a robbery call and get a message "come quick, Sally Ann did not pick up after her dog"? He laughed, everybody laughed, everybody but me.

I held up my hand and when recognized said, "all of you think this is amusing but you do not have to smell it, step in it and wear it to work." It was well known that the KPD did not intend to enforce the ordinance and they did not. I took a picture of a man who lived in the Sterchi who did not pick up after his two dogs. I had just gotten into my car to go to work when he came over and yelled at me. The whole time he was yelling his dogs were scratching my car door.

The damage was $700. I took pictures of the man, dogs and damaged car door as well as his name and address, and I took it to the KPD to ask how to proceed. The officer I spoke with said, "how do you know that the man in the apartment is the same man who did not pick up and his dogs scratched the car door?"

But my favorite story is I got a call saying, "it has finally happened." There was a Trolley full of tourists stopped on Walnut, at the corner of Walnut and Union. They watched a woman not pick-up after her dog and so did a bicycle officer. He asked her to pick-up. She refused. The officer asked the second time and she said (and I love it), "do you know who I am?" She was a judge's wife. The officer handed her a ticket and the whole trolley full of tourists broke out in a lusty applause.

The positive outcomes from all of this are: a non-profit was the first to install and maintain litter bag sites on the grassy area. The city followed suit and installed litterbags downtown. Then came the Dog parks and now Knoxville advertises itself as "Dog Friendly." I am still amazed that with a little help, time, and persistence good things can happen. After all this time I still run into to people who say: "well, there is the old Pooper Trooper."

The Blessing of the Pansies

Pansies

In 2000 George Walker Bush was elected the forty-third President of the United States of America. In the fall of 2000 I had helped Abby Conklin, who was the Assistant Basketball Coach at UNC Asheville, design changes for the locker room. I did not charge anything for my services and as payment was invited to travel with the team to Tallahassee to play Florida State in a pre-season game. We arrived in Tallahassee in the middle of the Hanging Chads Fiasco which also just happened to be the same weekend as the Florida vs Florida State football game. When we arrived at the hotel, we found that because of all the chaos our rooms were still occupied by journalists. We sat in the lobby all afternoon until the journalists were removed and we were allowed into the rooms.

Carol Evans, Patti Smith, and Diane Mack

Tallahassee is home to the Florida State Capitol, Florida State University and was a study in madness because of the Hanging Chads ballot re-count. The basketball game was played on Friday night and the football game on Saturday. We were the guest of the University at the football game and watched from Bobby Bowden's Terrace. I love college students because they surely do know how to enjoy events.

At the game some were painted head to toe, and others decked out in twinkle lights I loved the pageantry of the Seminoles horse and planting of the spear in mid-field before the start of the game. What does this have to do with "The Blessing of the Pansies"? After the trip to Tallahassee, I was at home looking out on the balcony where I had planted Pansies and thinking "there must be joy in Mudville somewhere" and the pansies said to me "Let us have a Blessing of the Pansies." We are pretty and bring joy." Any excuse for a party will do. I spoke with a few neighbors, and we thought a Blessing of the Pansies was exactly what we needed to raise our spirits. It was a very much spur of the moment affair. We decide a day – come as you are, after work and if you wanted something to drink- bring it.

There were no formal invitations just word-of-mouth and if it rains come anyway. Steve Dupree, a longtime downtown friend, was of course, our preferred Blesser. We gathered in the lobby and visited until we decided it was time for the blessing or until we could find Steve. Across the front of my unit are three French doors that serve as windows. We all went outside, with a beverage, and Steve stood in the middle window, one floor above the street. Steve is six feet, eight inches tall and filled the space. He is a wonderful speaker and writer, and so his blessing was perfect.

Pansies on Patti's Balcony, 120 S Gay St

Steve Dupree at the first Blessing of the Pansies on Oct. 29, 2004.

There have been nineteen years of blessings. The blessing took on a life of its own and over the years bloomed into a full-fledged party. The more who heard about it the more who wanted to come. Everybody was always welcome and they wanted to bring food. I always made chili and all the "fixings" to turn a bowl of chili into a "Petro." The name

"Petro" comes from "Petroleum", the theme of the 1982 World's Fair in Knoxville. The Petro was introduced during the World's Fair and was served in a Frito Bag. Fritos were the first layer, then chili, shredded cheese, sour cream, onions, salsa and jalapenos. Everybody served themselves but we used bowls not Frito bags. Besides dips, chips, and desserts we always had plenty of adult beverages, as well as water and soft drinks.

Susi Schaeffer

Gurny Barrett

After the first few years Jack O'Hanlon and Jerry Becker joined Dupree by adding their most unique style to the Blessing. Celebrity politicians joined: Madeline Rogero, the City Mayor and Tim Burchett, the County Mayor, but the big stars were my neighbors. Dupree, O'Hanlon, and Becker covered the religions: Dupree, a Protestant, O'Hanlon a Catholic, and Becker a Jew.

*Dupree, O'Hanlon, Becker, Mayor Rogero and me at
Blessing of the Pansies*

This was just fun. One Blessing, Carol Evans's dad and
his friend Miss Emily were visiting from Georgia. Carol
explained that her dad and Miss Emily could only stay a
short time for the Blessing, and she would take them home.
We were well into the party upstairs when I noticed that they
were seated on the sofa. Carol said they did not want to leave
and miss the fun. The precious little pansy became the reason
or excuse for friends and neighbors to get together once a
year. I hope we can continue.

Floral blessings bestowed

City gardener brings smiles with profusion of pansies

BY INA HUGHS
hughsi@knews.com

AMY SMOTHERMAN/NEWS SENTINEL

The Rev. Steve Dupree leans out of the apartment window of Gay Street resident Patti Smith to perform the Blessing of the Pansies. Smith's pansies keep the community's spirits up during the gray days of winter.

Patti Smith's garden is no secret. In fact, it's something of a legend in the 100th block of South Gay Street.

Every year when the weather turns warm, Smith fills her window boxes with portulaca, two stories above the street, and all spring and summer they dance there in the sun over a sea of asphalt and concrete.

And every fall, when pumpkins grin and goblins start to prowl — like clockwork, Smith says — "out go the portulaca and in go the pansies."

Thursday evening at sunset, Smith threw a party for her window boxes. She called it the Blessing of the Pansies, inviting her neighbors — and anybody else who wanted to come — to say a prayer for beauty and light, and afterward gather in the lobby of her apartment building for fun and fellowship "as long as the wine lasted."

The Rev. Steve Dupree, adorned with a crown of pansies and a happy smile, raised his arms to celebrate the goodness of neighborly love and the beauty turned loose in their community by this kind lady and her window box garden.

"Everybody's fussing and cussing," Smith says in explaining the occasion from her perspective. "I think about these pansies that just bob and shine all winter as if to remind us to stop and smile even when things get tough."

Smith's Blessing of the Pansies may not get as much press as the Blessing of the Shrimp Boats in Charleston or the Blessing of the Hounds in fox hunting circles, but to the folks on South Gay Street, it was a chance to salute the 126 red, yellow, white and purple pansies that will see them through the winter, bobbing their sassy heads in a world that so badly needs their brand of good cheer.

Smith has lived on South Gay Street for going on 10 years, and as more and more neighbors choose to live in the city, she is determined to keep her garden growing. "In wintertime, it's the only plant life around," Smith says.

Even the business community has come to count on those pansies. On gray, dark days, when the sky and the buildings all turn the same color, Smith's pansies perk up their colorful heads and cheer the whole neighborhood.

Ina Hughs may be reached at 865-342-6268.

The Blessing of the Pansies

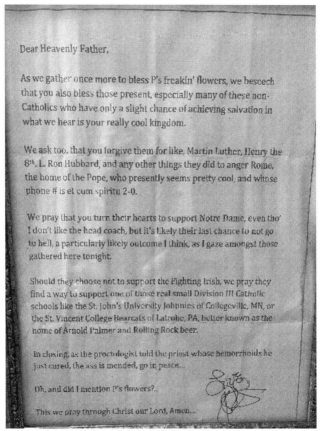

Dear Heavenly Father,

As we gather once more to bless P's freakin' flowers, we beseech that you also bless those present, especially many of these non-Catholics who have only a slight chance of achieving salvation in what we hear is your really cool kingdom.

We ask too, that you forgive them for like, Martin Luther, Henry the 8th, L. Ron Hubbard, and any other things they did to anger Rome, the home of the Pope, who presently seems pretty cool, and whose phone # is et cum spiritu 2-0.

We pray that you turn their hearts to support Notre Dame, even tho' I don't like the head coach, but it's likely their last chance to not go to hell, a particularly likely outcome I think, as I gaze amongst those gathered here tonight.

Should they choose not to support the Fighting Irish, we pray they find a way to support one of those real small Division III Catholic schools like the St. John's University Johnnies of Collegeville, MN, or the St. Vincent College Bearcats of Latrobe, PA, better known as the home of Arnold Palmer and Rolling Rock beer.

In closing, as the proctologist told the priest whose hemorrhoids he just cured, the ass is mended, go in peace...

Oh, and did I mention P's flowers?...

This we pray through Christ our Lord, Amen...

Jack O'Hanlon's blessing at the Blessing of the Pansies

NOTE: In 2022 we hosted the last Blessing in Knoxville.........In 2023 we had the first Blessing at the Cajun RV Park on the beach in Biloxi, Mississippi.

Ready for UT Bowl Game, 2021 Cajun RV Park,
Biloxi, Mississippi

The Power of Paint

Downtown Knoxville in the 1990's was just waking to the possibility of rebirth. Gay Street is the north-south corridor toward the river and is the hub of restaurants, hotels, shops and government. Knoxville has a dual governing system, the city and the county each has its own mayor. The city mayor and the county mayors are both housed on the river and on the same floor in the City-County Building. County dwellers pay county taxes, while city dwellers pay county taxes and city taxes, and downtown dwellers pay county, city and C.B.I.D taxes. C.B.I.D., now known as the Downtown Knoxville Alliance, supplies services the city cannot. The special assessment district covers 400 city blocks from the Old City to Volunteer Landing, to Eleventh Street to Hall of Fame Drive. This suggests lots of governing for all downtown dwellers. I think offices for all the governing needs filters much like furnace filters or maybe explicit names for departments. Names like "Petty Laws" and "Rules Department," or "Just Because I Can Office."

In 1998 two attorneys, who were married, had their law office in their condo on the west side of Gay Street in the 100 Block. In front of their office was a yellow curb and it was yellow almost to the corner of the block so that no parking was allowed in front of their office. On the east side of the street, across from their office, parking was allowed almost to the corner of the block. The lawyer's theory was that because they defended police officers against the city this was retaliation from the city.

What made this so egregious was that three blocks down the street vehicles could park, almost to the corner, in the most congested corner of entire the street.

Beginning here the story will be told through the eyes of the Citizen. The Citizen was a resident in the same block as the lawyers. He/She recognized the unfairness and set out to right a wrong. This could not have turned out better. One Sunday morning the Citizen spray painted the yellow curb in front of the lawyer's office with gray spray paint. This equalized the parking spaces on both sides of the street. As the Citizen was painting a few neighbors walked by. They did not stop or speak, just nodded and moved on. About a week after the curb turned gray the City Traffic Division People showed up. Nobody knew what was going on and nobody asked. A few days later the traffic people were back.......... are you ready? Drum Roll Please!!!!!! They installed two parking meters which are still in operation twenty - three years later. The Citizen strongly feels that the revenue earned from those two meters should be deducted from his/her property tax.

All was well and good, and the neighborhood was full of slight smiles and the feeling was just this side of righteous until the Citizen got a phone call. The Assistant Chief of Police was calling to point out that painting a city curb was against the law and would not be tolerated. He also said that it would cost the city $200 to repaint the curb.

The Citizen wanted to reply "no, the two cans only cost a dollar fifty each at the Dollar General, thus demonstrating the Power of Paint.

A Tree Was Planted on Tyson Street

I owned a sign shop on Tyson Street across from the Old Gray Cemetery. Next door was Ernie's sign shop, and I would hire his employees to help me install jobs that were too heavy or needed special equipment. For years I had worked for the University of Tennessee Athletics Department. One job that happened each year was the Lady Vols Hall of Fame Induction. The university had 14"X14" plaques printed with the inductee's name and biographical information. The Lady Vol offices were in Stokely Hall, and we installed the plaques on the hall wall that ran between the coach's offices. When the installation was complete, we covered the plaques with brown paper. Donna Thomas oversaw the Induction Ceremony and part of the lead-up to the dinner was to walk the inductees down the hall to view their plaques. The plaques were uncovered just before the formal presentation to the inductees.

The wall was made of painted concrete block and was hard to drill into, so I would hire one of Ernie's employees to do the drilling. We used a Hammer Drill. I did not own a Hammer Drill, and even if I did it was too heavy for me to hold head-high and drill. I asked Ernie to rent me one of his men for Thursday. He did not have anybody available but said, Bob, his neon man's son, Jake, had just moved here from Alabama with a friend and maybe they could help. Jake agreed and I picked him up on Thursday morning. On the way to Stokely I asked about his dad. Ernie had told me he was worried about Bob because on Monday afternoon he got a call and needed to go home but would be back. He did not call nor return to work Tuesday, Wednesday, or Thursday morning. Jake said his dad was fine but did not make any explanation other than his dad was "fine."

We met Donna and were given installation instructions. Jake started to drill, and he smelled awful. So bad that I went upstairs to the souvenir shop and bought a tee shirt off the five-dollar clearance rack. I loved the tee shirt because on the front it said, "Will Rogers never met a man he did not like" and on the back it said, "Will Rogers never met Steve Spurrier." Jake did not appreciate the shirt as much as I did but he put it on. It was not Jake's shirt that smelled so bad, it was Jake. The Hammer Drill made a huge noise, so we tried to be as efficient as possible. Job done, I drove him back to Ernie's and later he came by to pick up his check

As Paul Harvey used to say, "and now for the rest of the story." On Monday Ernie told me about Bob. He went home because of a domestic problem involving his son and daughter but never returned to work. On Friday Ernie learned there had been a fight between Jake and his dad, and his dad was killed. Jake and his friend had rolled Bob in a shower curtain and dumped him on the bank of Douglas Lake where he was discovered on Friday.

Ernie was distraught. He loved Bob and said he was a good man, a skilled worker, and had tried to be a good father. In Bob's honor, Ernie planted a tree on Tyson Street.

Rest in Peace, Little Fetus

I live on the east side of the 100 Block of Gay Street. The building to the south was undergoing renovation and the workmen were cleaning out the bottom floor. The floor was one-hundred years old, fine dirt, and had a four-foot concrete wall at the back.

On top of the wall was a clear glass bottle about ten inches tall with a cork in the opening. Hanging inside the bottle was something. The workmen showed me the bottle and asked if I knew what it was. I had no idea.

My neighbor, Sally, who was on the faculty at the University of Tennessee Veterinary School, was walking down the street. I stopped her, showed her the bottle and ask if this could be human. She said she did not know but possibly it could be.

I called Dr. Bass's office. He is the founder of the internationally known Body Farm here in Knoxville at the university. He sent a young man over to see what we had found. He told me it most likely was human. Under law he had to take it to the University of Tennessee Hospital and report found human remains so it could be disposed of properly.

I began to try to find out what had happened and why this was in this building. I found out that the building had been used as a medical equipment business. The only information I could find was that apparently the Fetus was stillborn, put into the bottle, hung by a thread and filled with a preservative liquid.

Over the years the preservative had evaporated, leaving the Fetus hanging. This, then could be sold to a medical school as a study tool.

I never could find out exactly what happened to the little fetus after it was turned into the university hospital. Rest in peace little Fetus.

Knoxville Journal Closed but Not Betty Bean

Patti and Bean in Old City, 2012

In 1991 the 106-year-old Knoxville Journal newspaper closed, putting sixty-nine employees out of work. One of these was Betty Bean, a well-known journalist. Bean had a going away party at HooRay's in the Old City and a lawyer friend came by to wish her well. He gave $10 and his keys to the valet. He went inside to tell Bean he couldn't stay and told her he had asked the valet to park his car upfront because he had to leave. Bean said, "what valet?" He went back outside to find the valet, but both the man and the car were gone.

The lawyer had a court appointment the next morning, and all his files were in the trunk of the car. He didn't want his friends to know what had happened, but he had to tell the judge. His car was found that afternoon in East Knoxville, bone dry, but all his files were still there.

Oh No, Please Not a Medical Alert Safety Device!

I have Medicare and supplemental medical insurance. A few years ago, my insurance company sent me a Medical Alert Safety device for free. The purpose of the device is to alert the company if the customer has a health-related emergency. This must be worn on a string around the neck so it will be able to send an alert in case of medical emergency. This is monitored 24/7. If there has been no activity in a prescribed amount of time, there will be a "wellness phone call."

I was still working at the time and would forget to wear it. Periodically I would get a phone call to check on my state of health. One night I was sound asleep and got a phone call from Knoxville Police Officer at my front door. I lived at 120 S. Gay Street in the commerce building in a condo. I had to get up, dress, walk down twenty-two steps because we had no elevator to open the door for the officer. The device people had called KPD and asked them to do a "wellness check" on me in the middle of the night. My reply was, "thank you officer for checking on me, sorry for your trouble."

But this was not the worst time. The absolute worst time occurred on a workday morning. It was early, probably seven a.m., and I was getting ready to take a shower. I sleep in a T-shirt and underwear and was ready to strip when I heard a noise in the front of my unit. I walked down to check out the noise —-and folks——I could not make this up—— standing in my living room were four Fire Fighters in complete firefighter gear: coats, hats and satchels. They had gotten a call to do a "wellness check." Please understand that, at this point I am a seventy-something year-old female standing in my living room with four fire fighters IN MY T-SHIRT AND UNDERWEAR. They have a key to get into buildings. I heard nothing until they were in my living room. They could not see most of me but certainly could tell I was up and moving about. I apologized for their trouble, they left and I called the company.

I was told that they called me, but when I did not answer they called the Fire Department. I said, "you never called me." They said that they did, and I said, "well, I have an iPhone that records all incoming and outgoing calls…I can prove you did not call me, can you prove you did?" My last question was: "how do I return this infernal DEVICE?"

NOTE: I know these devices are helpful and needed but I was too busy at the time to care.

No Eggs in the Building

Our building is on the 100 Block of Gay Street. It was built in 1896 and is seven stories tall. In the early 1900s trains were coming to our town and were impeded by a viaduct at the end of our block. In order to accommodate train traffic, the viaduct needed to be raised. In doing so the first three floors of our building were left below street level. To afford residents' light, all three floors have large, one plate windows. The building is one-hundred feet from the street to the alley.

When developers bought the building in 1991, they divided all floors into two units, one facing Gay Street and one facing the alley except for the fourth floor which is street level and had always been commercial. The first-floor owner only built-out the front unit. The second and third floors were originally sold as two units each but, later, were combined into one unit, street to alley. The fifth, sixth and seventh floors are two units each.

I needed to explain the building lay-out because this is where the eggs come in. Two times eggs have caused a fire, one in the second-floor unit and one last night in the first-floor unit. The egg burner, in each case, opened the door to let out the smoke and this set off the excruciatingly loud alarm. The Fire Department was two blocks away and arrived instantly. Two fire trucks arrived with eight fire fighters. Once again, they saved the building but not the eggs.

A neighbor who just recently moved here from California could not believe two fire trucks would respond to put out eggs. Mark, my upstairs neighbor, and I explained that all these buildings in the 100 Block are over one-hundred years old. She said, "But the building is brick." We explained that the interior is wood----wood that is over one-hundred years old, and if one building catches on fire, it will threaten the whole block.

In the future maybe we should ban egg-cooking on the lower levels.

Who Does Not Love a Snow Day?

Snowy Day on 100 Block of Gay St

Downtown is a wonderful place to live. The number one block in the city is the 100 Block of Gay Street, in our opinion. A lot of people do not realize that we are a neighborhood, but we are, and we love it. We meet on the street, catchup on family, friends and pets, go for a meal or a drink. Go to movies, plays, and concerts right here in our neighborhood. One of our favorite days is "Snow Days."

This was in 2011 or 2012. When it snowed, not much, but enough that Krogers ran out of everything immediately and of course nobody could go to work or church but could always party. Our neighborhood group was Susi and Greg, Leigh and Gene, Trish and Buzz, Melinda and Butch, Toni, Kim Henry, me and one not-nice man. On Snow Days we met at noon at CRU, which was in the 100 Block, and always stayed a while. One day stands out as memorable. Trish and Buzz were out-of-town, and I was feeding their cat.

Our Snow Day crew was at CRU and I told them I had to go feed the cat and of course they all volunteered to help. It was snowy and icy, but being the adventurers we were, we made it all the way to the next block. The cat was in the basement, all alone, and we decided Cat also needed a vacation. Susi volunteered to keep her until the owners returned. Once more, being the valiant snow warriors, we made it back to CRU. Susi placed Cat in her bathroom. She and Greg lived next door to CRU in David Dewhurst's "Boat Condo." All of us went into CRU and ordered a beverage while we waited for Susi to place Cat. It was not pretty. Cat did not like her new home in the bathroom and did not much like Susi. When Susi returned to the festivities downstairs, she had multiple scratches to prove it. We should have gotten a clue because Cat fought all the way down the street. Since Cat was in the bathroom and did not appreciate being there. Susi and Greg only used the bathroom when absolutely necessary.

We always had fun on snow days. One time we were down on the viaduct for some kind of ceremony but I cannot remember what it was or why we chose to make it part of our snow day. Must have been fun or why would I sort-of remember?

Danny Mayfield...Was it Mean or Just Plain Evil?

Looking back to 2001, Knoxville City Council took a vote that shocked the conscience of the city. If you think the political atmosphere is bad now, you should have been here in 2001.

Danny Mayfield came from Camden, New Jersey, to attend Knoxville College in 1989 and on the bus ride down he met Missy Chisholm from Philadelphia, Pennsylvania, whom he later married. Danny was Valedictorian and graduated Summa Cum Laude.

After college Danny, along with Chris Woodhull, founded Tribe One, an inner-city youth ministry.

In 1997 he ran for Knoxville City Council, Sixth district. The sixth district covered neighborhoods which includes Mechanicsville and Kendrick Place in the west to Burlington in the east, Parkridge to the north down to Delrose in the south. This district was predominately black. Danny was black and ran a grassroots campaign. In an upset victory he won over incumbent William "Bill" Powell.

In February of 2000, he was diagnosed with bone cancer. Missy has a Master's Degree in Plant and Soil Science from University of Tennessee. She attended council meetings with Danny so she could help him stay informed on issues. Between meetings she would check information on current issues so he could make voting decisions. March 22, 2001, Danny Mayfield died at the age of thirty-two.

City Council had thirty days to name someone to serve out Danny's term that ended in nine months in December. On April 3, 2001, Missy asked the city council "to do the right thing" by selecting her to serve out the nine months left of Danny's term. Council members were District 1 Gary Underwood, District 2 Jean Teague, District 3 Ivan Harmon, District 4 Carlene Malone, District 5 Larry Cox, District 6 Danny Mayfield, deceased. At-Large members: Seat A Jack Sharp also Vice Mayor, Seat B Nick Pavlis, and Seat C Ed Shouse. Nick Pavlis made the motion to allow Missy to serve and Carlene Malone seconded the motion. The motion failed six to two. It was a rowdy meeting.

This is when it all "hit the fan." Council voted not to allow Missy to serve the nine months. Normally, this is a courtesy afforded to the spouse of a deceased member. I could not find information of this ever having been done in Knoxville. City Council appointed Raleigh Wynn, Sr., a seventy-seven-year-old teacher and coach instead.

The sixth district constituents were outraged and discussed what could be done. Neighbors decided that the only solution was a recall of some council members. Steve Dupree filed the Knox Recall petition. He said," "I do not think they have left us any choice whatsoever.". The Election Commission had to approve wording and form of petition. The commission said that fifteen percent of registered voters were needed to go forward with putting a recall on the ballot in September. Fifteen percent translates into 15,700 signatures. City Law Director, Michael Kelley, deposed Councilmen Sharp, Shouse and Cox and from Knox Recall Diana Conn, Steve DuPree, Regina Rizzi, Brent

Minchey and Greg Ganus. Margaret Held was attorney for Knox Recall. The recall was allowed to go forward but were unable to get 15,700 signatures. There are reports that some would not sign the petition because of fear of retaliation at work.

A reporter asked council members why they voted against Missy Mayfield. Member replies:

Jack Sharp said, "She's got those two kids, and she needs to stay home and take care of them."

Ivan Harmon said, "I'm afraid she is going to be a Carlene Malone clone."

Jean Teague said, "I don't know her."

Unnamed member said, "would call Alvin Nance and get Missy a job."

EULOGY

Danny brought wonderful gifts to our city and to our city council. Danny brought us the future. He respected the past and its lessons, but Danny clearly embodied our future. Our Generation X Council Member, Danny began his council career by introducing additions to the usual dress code of government officials. His wardrobe was immediately noticed. It symbolized change: different ideas, different expectations, different ways of thinking, a different approach, and a different future for our city.

Danny brought a laptop computer to council meetings. Again, it was noticed. It reminded us all of the impact of the information age and the power of information in bringing about social change. And it told us that we are not going back.

Danny brought us the gift of youth. Youth is filled with hope and energy, enthusiasm and idealism, and passion. He brought all of this to his council work. And, just like his wardrobe, and his laptop, his idealism was noticed.

But, the exuberance of youth was directed by Danny. Life had already tested him. He had faced adversity and had emerged with JOY NOT BITTERNESS. With COURAGE NOT FEAR. With STRENGTH NOT WEAKNESS.

From his experience he earned the gifts of peace and joy. And he brought those gifts to every council meeting and to every council task. And his grace was noticed. This was obvious during the good times and, more importantly, during the not-so-good times. His joyous and peaceful presence comforted and strengthened his supporters and disarmed and challenged his critics. It reminded everyone that we must work on what truly is important.

Danny brought us many wonderful gifts. He was our brief glimpse of the future—— and it was very beautiful.

March 24, 2001

With love and respect for Danny Mayfield, Council Member, 6th District

From Carlene Malone, Council Member 4th District

After all was said and done, Danny was dead. His work was over, and Missy was not allowed to carry forward and put closure to his work. However, he was not forgotten.

A billboard by Lamar Advertising put up, for ten days on I-40, reading" "DANNY, THANK YOU FOR TOUCHING

OUR LIVES" and on November 2, 2004, there was a ribbon cutting ceremony for the DANNY MAYFIELD PARK in Mechanicsville.

Recall megaphone

Friends

The 1961 R.O.T.C Ball – The Best Ball Ever

In 1959, I was a student at Middle Tennessee State University, thirty miles south of Nashville in a rural area. When I say "rural" area I mean there were cows grazing next to the dormitory. I was there to pull up my grades so I could be initiated into the sorority at the University of Tennessee in Knoxville.

R.O.T.C (pronounced RotCee) stands for Reserve Officers' Training Corp. Their goal is to train college students for future service in the U.S. military. The Ball was in honor of the school's mascot, Nathan Bedford Forrest, a Confederate War hero. By Springtime and Ball-time I was ready to join in the merriment. Our ball party included Eddie Bissell, John Briggs and John Telliferro, all pharmacy students at the University of Tennessee School of Pharmacy in Memphis. Patty and Marcia were my two roommates.

M.T.S.U. student enrollment was three thousand and U.T was thirteen thousand. M.T.S.U.'s campus was run by six girls who were prettier, smarter and cooler than any of us. For instance, the way they dressed for football games was a marvel. At U.T footwear fashion was Keds (canvas lace ups) with lots of holes, which is casual dress. Also, the girls at U.T. carried large purses so that their date had some place to carry his fifth of liquor. Not these girls – they wore

110

"church clothes" to the ballgames. I may be remembering incorrectly, but I think some of the girls wore gloves—white gloves—and they all wore high heel pumps, and it goes without saying, meticulous bouffant-piled-high hair. Well anyway, all the rest of us, not of the "we-run this-place" crowd, just watched while they ran the campus, which included the R.O.T.C. Ball held each Spring.

I called Bissell and told him I would provide formal dress. Patty, Marcia and I went to Nashville and rented three Antebellum Gowns and three Confederate Uniforms. So, with us in our exceptionally beautiful gowns and the guys in handsome uniforms, we arrived at the Ball. We toured the Gym (this is where the Ball was held). Mostly folks did not speak to us – just stared. We stayed long enough to have our pictures taken several times. We obviously had offended the "ruling party" in their perfect dresses, perfect dates, and all were in the process of collecting their due of "job-well-done-for-Ball-planning." Did we steal their thunder and supreme moment in history? Yes, we did and I loved it – still do.

Patti McPeters and Eddie Bissell

After being assured we had been seen by all – we left – changed clothes - and went to Printer's Alley in downtown Nashville. Printer's Alley was all bars – still is.

We spent most of the night in Nashville and the next day we drove to Percy Priest Lake. The day was overcast and so were we. We did not stay long.

On the drive back to Murfreesboro the boys sat in the front seat and we girls sat in the back seat. We girls were not speaking, just listening to the boys discuss last week's assignment, which was learning to make suppositories. One said, "yours was long and skinny" and the reply was "yours was round and lumpy."

Perfect ending to the 1961 R.O.T.C Ball – Best Ball Ever.

Summer Work

Summer of 1960

Before you enter the adult workforce there are two seasons...School and Summer.

Back in the 1950s I do not remember girls working during the summer vacation. At least, I did not work summers until I was in college. I entered the University of Tennessee in the Fall of 1958, joined a sorority, and learned to smoke and drink beer like all the smart girls. I loved college life and everything about it: sleeping in, football games, and pizza at the Quarterback on Cumberland. The one thing I failed to do was to take my studies seriously. For a sorority pledge to be initiated into membership she must make good grades for two consecutive terms. I did not make my grades, so it was suggested, by the sorority, that I transfer to Middle Tennessee State College in Murfreesboro, Tennessee, south of Nashville. I was to pull up my grades and transfer back to UT. I was majoring in psychology at Tennessee but MTSU did not have enough hours for a minor, so I switched to Physical Education. It was more fun anyway. MTSU was a small school of 3,000 students.

On the lobby bulletin board was a summer camp counselor job application. I applied and was hired as a waterfront and swimming instructor at Point O 'Pines Camp for Girls on Brant Lake in upstate New York. The camp catered to wealthy New York girls, most of whom were Jewish. My cabin backed up to the lake. The camp site was originally an island but was filled in and became a peninsula. The cabins were built with the backs to the lake and the cabin fronts facing a large grassy area. The dining hall was up on a hill and the recreation hall was down the hill to the waterfront. The Rec Hall served as a Bingo Chamber, Theater, Play Stage and general usage space. The swimming area of the lake was built with wooden walkways out into the water that separated the three swimming areas. There was a tall slide anchored out in the deepest swim area. The canoes were tied up next to the Rec Hall. The camp was a good and had a functional design. At the opposite end of the campus were a Craft House and Tennis Courts. The campers' schedules were flexible in that they could choose activities except everybody had to take swimming.

The staff was allowed one day off each week and could leave camp after lights out unless you were on duty. On Duty, or O.D., meant that you were sit in a chair, under a light, and be responsible for the campers in six cabins. O.D. was kind of like today's 911… yell if you need help. There was a boy's camp one mile up the road with an old tavern in the middle of the mile. We were allowed to go to the tavern and so were the boy's counselors. The most exciting part of camp that summer was the effort to catch a Peeping Tom. It took three nights to catch him. Our Waterfront Director was a 6'4" football player from the University of North Carolina and was not afraid of much. The Peeper came in by canoe, was caught and turned over to local law enforcement and the campers never knew anything about him.

The most embarrassing moment happened when the camp owners invited me and another counselor to sit at their table during dinner. They invited counselors each week-day night. We were served big pieces of chicken. The piece of chicken was so big it took up half of the plate. The other counselor was sitting next to me and speaking across the table to the owners when suddenly, her piece of chicken jumped right off her plate and into her lap. I did not do it but was embarrassed for her because that is the kind of thing that happens to me and I knew how she felt.

We could borrow a camp vehicle on days off for excursions to Saratoga to the racetrack and to visit the White Mountains in Vermont, but my favorite was breakfast at Schultze's. Schultze was a counselor whose parents owned a large Victorian house on a small, private island one mile from camp. She would invite two or three buddies to breakfast on our days off and we would canoe over. This was the first time in my life I had been served breakfast by a maid in someone's house. Breakfast served by a maid...I could hardly believe it. Schulze's folks owned a winter house in Queens, and we were invited down after camp for a few days and had dinner at Mama Leone's in Manhattan. After Queens, the next time I saw Schultze was in Amsterdam

Schultze was a student at Brandeis's University and was on a summer study abroad program. Two friends and I had gone to Amsterdam for the weekend. We had traveled by train and there was a bicycle rental shop across from the train station. We were standing at this curved counter waiting to get information when I looked down the counter and saw a ring I recognized. It was Schultze and she told me their next stop after Amsterdam was Paris. As it turned out she was being housed in the Netherlands. How about that for coincidences?

Summer of 1961

My roommate at MTSU was Marcia and she had been to Paris, France as an exchange student in a summer work program in 1960. She told me about the program, I applied and was accepted into the program headquartered in Louisville, Kentucky. June 20, 1961, I reported for orientation. During orientation we were given our work assignments and information about the company and employer. But a large part of the message was, "Do Not Be A Bad American." We were told many of the things that insult the French and to not do them. Most important was: "eat everything on your plate," "Do not use ketchup," and "Always try to speak French." We were given the schedule for the first week in Paris, which included receptions, meet and greets, tours, and a home visit.

We were housed on the campus of the City University. We were supposed to stay in the United States House, but it was bombed by the Cubans, probably because of the Bay of Pigs incident, so we lived in the Netherlands' House. The first meal we had on campus, a student came in and everybody started throwing hard rolls at him. I never did find out what that was about. In the Netherlands' house we had rules. Do not hang wet underwear in your room, hang it in the laundry room which I did, and it was stolen. Outside doors were locked at 9:00 p.m. but you could get in if you paid the Concierge. Hot chocolate and a roll were served off the lobby early in the morning. The hot chocolate was thick and made with real chocolate.

Dennis and I were paired for the home visit where we were served dinner. Our hosts were a young couple and their baby. The menu was a thick slice of pork covered in gravy and vegetables. The pork had a half-inch ring of fat and I cannot eat fat. Because we had spent so much time learning to not be an Ugly American, I had a dilemma. If I did not eat the fat our hosts would be insulted, and I had eaten everything but the fat. The couple each left the table, one to get dessert and the other to check on the baby. I told Dennis, "I cannot eat this fat," and he shoved it all in his mouth and had it eaten by the time our hosts returned to the table.

International insult avoided. I asked Dennis what I could do as "Pay Back" and he said, "go to mass with me." So, I did. We went to an old cathedral, sat in saggy, woven bottom chairs and the service was either in Latin or French. For a lifelong Baptist I felt as if I had paid a lot forward.

This pretty much covered our first week of activities, and now to work. My job was at Crystal et Bronze. They manufactured crystal and bronze cigarette jars, ashtrays, cigarette lighters, and lamps. I worked in the office and my first job was to update their pricing catalog by converting the French franc into the currency of their customers, German, English, Italian, etc. The next job was to go to all the tobacco shops in the neighborhood and collect change and to make deliveries. In Paris, everything closes from noon to two for lunch. I delivered small packages and /or letters. Transportation was the Metro, of which I understood little. In Strawberry Plains we did not have one single underground train. I got lost, the businesses were closed, I missed lunch, got on wrong trains, but all-in-all learning experiences are called education.

My best friends were Dudley Burgess from Frankfort, Kentucky, and Anne Huddleston from Harrodsburg, Kentucky. They were both students at Centre College in Danville, Kentucky. In Paris, Dudley worked in a grocery store and Anne worked in a bank. We worked from 8:00 a.m. to 6:00 p.m. with two hours off for lunch. After work, by the time we got home, had something to eat it was 9:00 p.m. and time to go out. During the week we would mostly go to Montmartre, which is a hill village in the center of Paris. The cobble stone streets were a path to museums, art centers, and the Sacre-Coeur Basilica on top of the hill. We met artists and gentle neighborhood people who were kind to us. We also went to Cavos, which were downstairs bars. I think the word Cavo means cable in French but that is what we called those bars. Music could always be heard outside and they mostly played Piaf songs.

On the weekend we would visit historical sites close to Paris as well as in- town sites. Edith Piaf was the rage in 1961. She was like our Judy Garland. On passing a Cavo you could hear a Piaf song. I had ticket to go to an outdoor Edith Piaf Concert, but she became incapacitated (that happened a lot), and the concert was cancelled. My favorite song was and is "Non, Je ne regretta rein." My exchange partner was Gilbert Bertrane and while he was here in Knoxville, he worked for TV channel ten and his job was to introduce the Early Show that came on at 4:00 p.m. in the afternoon. When I returned to Knoxville, he gave me a CD with complete works of Edith Piaf. After we completed our work obligation, Dudley, Anne, and I decided to hitch hike across Europe, which was safe at that time. We each packed a backpack and stored our luggage in Paris. We had our own rules of the road while hitchhiking. One, we would always travel together. Two, we would be well-groomed at all times. Our trip got off to a late start because I had gone to London and Edinburgh the week before and was to be back in Paris by 7:00 p.m. Friday night. I was to meet the girls at a bar at 7:00 p.m. because they moved out of the Netherlands' House on Friday and into a hotel. When I left Paris, they had not yet decided on a hotel and that is why we were meeting at a bar. On the flight into Paris, we circled Orly Airfield several times before the pilot announced that we were returning to London because he could not tell if the landing gear was locked into place. The flight back to London was to use up fuel. We landed safely and were taken into a terminal where we sent wires to those in Paris who were expecting us. I sent a wire to Dudley and Anne at the bar but they never heard from me, so they left. I arrived at the bar about 10:30 p.m., they were gone, and I waited until midnight and got to the hotel around the corner. Keep in mind that this was thirty years before cell phones, so I had no way to contact them. I spent Saturday and Sunday looking for them and nights at a "not good" hotel. The one-star type. At this point I had little money because I took what I needed for London and Edinburgh and left the rest of my cash with them… this was way before credit and debit cards so we traveled on cash. Monday morning, I went to the bank where Anne had worked and found her boyfriend who remembered the name of the hotel where they were. I found them about noon, and they were doing their nails and hair and were not the least bit concerned about me. I truly looked like "Death Warmed Over." The next day we began our Hitch-Hiking Adventure.

From August 2, 1961 to August 26, 1961 these are the towns we visited in order: GERMANY – Toul, Munich, Bicol, Garmisch, Innsbruck. (Paris to Innsbruck, 700 miles in six days). ITALY – Venice, Florence, Rome, Sorrento. FRANCE – Nice. MONTE CARLO. SWITZERLAND – Interlaken. August twenty-fifth, we arrived in Paris to board the plane for home on August 26, 1961.

Summer of 1962—Southern California

Marcia had worked at the Flying Butler Restaurant in Newport Beach, California in the summer of 1961. She was hired back for summer of 1962; she recommended me and I was hired. We rented an apartment in Huntington Beach. We had been there a few days when, Nancy, whom I had grown up with showed up, unannounced, to spend the summer with us. Marcia and I worked in Newport Beach and Nancy got a job in Mesa. I owned the only car. Marcia and I worked at the same place, but Nancy worked fifteen miles in the opposite direction. This was a problem. I was Nancy's chauffer. It was not good and I was not happy. I got home from work one day to find Nancy sitting by the pool and she asked, "did you get my medicine?" I said "no, take my car and you can go to the drug store." She did and on the way back wrecked my precious little Hillman. I loved that little car. It was a light blue English Hillman with a dark gray convertible top. A dealership in Knoxville had the Hillman on the show floor and I have no idea why they had this strange little car. The wrecked Hillman was put in a repair garage where it stayed for six weeks. I was given a dark-green, awful, ugly, dirty piece of not-cool car. It is hard to look cool in a not-cool car.

We worked and went to the beach. Bull fights in Tijuana were always an adventure because they usually started at The Worlds' Longest Bar. Los Angeles was intimidating, but I enjoyed the wonder of Hollywood. We were there during all the coverage of the tragedy of Marilyn Monroe's death. I was dating Gary, whose folks lived on a canal in Newport Beach. His Dad had a boat shaped like a submarine and was named the Naughtylass. We would go out on the Naughtylass to fish, but mostly we just waited on them. Fishing in the ocean is not easy. Drinking is not either. If you set a drink on the deck of the submarine and it tilted, off went your beverage into the drink.

I had to be back in Knoxville to report to UT to begin student teaching. We had finally gotten my car back so we could make the trip home. Nancy had gone back to Knoxville to get ready for school. From Huntington Beach we went to Las Vegas. Back in those days winnings were paid in silver dollars. We won enough to pay for gas all the way home and we paid with silver dollars. We had just driven into West Tennessee when a big storm hit. The windshield wipers had quit working several days ago. The problem was we could not stop for the storm because I was just barely going to make it back to UT on time. So, this is what we did. We put the top down on the car because as-long- as we were driving the rain just flew overhead and not in the car. One drove and the other stood in the seat, leaned over and wiped the rain off the windshield with a tea towel, tee shirt or anything we could find so the driver could see. Marcia lived in Bell Buckle, Tennessee, which is southwest of Nashville. Sometime before we got to Bell Buckle, a rock broke a headlight. I dropped off Marcia and drove on into Knoxville. I guess we did not earn any style- points but you have got to give us credit for: "never quit until you are done.

Summer 1963—The Movies

I graduated from the University of Tennessee, June 2, 1963, with a B.S. in Education and a double major in physical education and health and a minor in English Literature. In May it dawned on me that nobody was beating down the door to hire me. I went by the UT Placement Center and found a teaching position open at Gulf Park College in Gulfport, Mississippi. I applied, was hired, and reported in August for my first big girl job.

I needed something to do from June second until the last week in August. So, I worked for my mother. She owned Helma's Restaurant and was catering meals to the movie set of "Fool Killer" starring Anthony Perkins. She needed help and I needed a job. This job consisted of delivering breakfast food and drink to the set in Chilhowee Park in East Knoxville or to the bus at the Andrew Johnson Hotel on Gay Street if they were going on location to the mountains,

Townsend or a farm somewhere in the middle of nowhere. Helma and I would deliver and serve lunch or dinner or both depending on the shooting schedule, we would arrive and be set up by whatever time we were told and then in a lot of cases sit and wait one to two hours. Serving food to a movie set is a lot of hurrying up and waiting.

The movie business is highly controlled by Unions. Included in the breakfast delivery was an insulated ten-gallon coffee urn I needed to put on the table but was too heavy for me to lift. A great big man was sitting in a chair watching and finally he got out of his chair and said, "the Union is not going to like this but let me help you." I was not going to drink the coffee, but his help was greatly appreciated, albeit illegal.

Driving food around three times a day to different locations is not without mishaps. One day we had driven forever to get to a remote farm and were told to set up in a cow pasture. We got everything set up only to realize that somebody had left the flatware. That somebody was me. I drove those tiny little, crooked, country back roads like a maniac stopping at anyplace that would have plasticware. I finally collected enough for the meal and nobody knew but mom and me. Oh Lord! I still break out in chills when I remember. Another mishap occurred while we were driving through a construction site. Thank goodness my mom was driving because she had to drive over a drop-off with a little curve. The bounce caused the Hot Box doors to pop open and we spilled creamed corn and green beans. My Mom always took more food that she thought she would need to

123

make sure everybody got enough. We sure made a mess though.

The movie people loved my mom because she went out of her way to pay attention to likes and not likes. She had catered to the movie set, "All the Way Home", filmed here in Knoxville. It was the James Agee Story starring Robert Preston. Years later she was in New York and went to see Mr. Preston in a play. He invited her backstage after the performance and told her he would have substituted her name for the name in the script but would have confused the other players.

A lot of words about working four summers. I have thoroughly enjoyed allowing my memory to pull forth many things I thought I had forgotten.

The Sands and Times Do Change

How do four young mothers, eight children, one maid, and one drop-in husband spend one week at the beach together?

Mothers and children: Casey and nine-month twins - Lee and Lou, Nancy and three-year-old Tracey and three-month-old Mary Barlette, Jerri and three-year-old Sherry and five-year-old Chris, I, one year old Adam, and seven-year-old Solon. The mothers went to school at the University of Tennessee. Casey, Jerri and I were sorority sisters and Nancy was Patti's roommate.

After graduation we all became working adults; Casey was an investigative newspaper reporter, Nancy worked in the family business, Jerri was an executive secretary and I was a gym teacher. After we graduated and became employed, we, as all southern women, were expected to get married, have babies and we did… We were living the dream.

The "dream" is full of mundane chores taking care of house, baby, husband, yard, church, family, Easter out-fits and Christmas pageants.

The beach is sunny, warm, beautiful and the house is available. My mother owned a house on Daytona Beach in Ponce Inlet, Florida.

What a great idea! Let's go to the beach! In addition to the mothers and children, Nancy, brought her maid, Mattie. Thank goodness.

We established a daily routine – everybody up, fed and to the beach. Run and fun in the water, sand and sun and then

125

back to the house for lunch in the courtyard. After lunch for
the children came beach for the mothers. Mattie was the
child watcher. Late afternoon back to the beach, supper, play
in the courtyard and in bed by 8:00 p.m. After the house was
quiet the grownups, in night gowns and lotion, would make
drinks and talk. Drink of choice; Casey – Bourbon, Jerri –
Gin, Nancy – Rum, and Patti – Scotch. We served ourselves
so we were generous.

All the little ones were in bed except three-year-old
Tracy. Her normal bedtime was whenever her parents went
to bed, even if it was mid-night. Some nights we stayed up
later than others which means we drank more. We kept the
liquor above the microwave. I had noticed that the Bourbon
and Rum bottles were emptier than the Gin and Scotch
bottles. I was drinking Scotch and Jerri was drinking Gin, so,
I asked Jerri if she thought Nancy and Casey were drinking
too much?

After two days we decided Mattie needed a break, so we
took her to the inlet to fish. She came back all excited
because she had met "a really nice man." She was married
and we asked her if her husband would be concerned about
her new friend and she said, "you know he has a bad heart
and you always need a backup." Come to find out that Mattie
had been imbibing all week, anytime we were out of the
house. I cannot really blame her. Mystery solved.

Jerri's husband, Bruce, had flown down for a one - day
business meeting in Orlando and he suggested a trip to
Disney World. Nancy and Jerri took the four older children.
Casey, Mattie, and I stayed home with the babies. This story
is like a coin, it has two sides.

Bruce dropped off the two mothers, four children and two strollers at Disney. He went to his meeting, picked up the Disney goers and returned to Daytona. What a different picture the "goers" and the "stay-at-homers" presented. I will never forget that Nancy left in her crisp, white, parquet sundress with red trim and returned looking as if she had been playing Rugby. Jerri just looked dazed. Something about a combination of crowds, kids, strollers, and the tram. The children had a great time. Casey and I were seated on the living room floor folding a mountain of towels and related how the babies had cried all day. Not true, but we did not want to point out how quiet, cool and comfortable we had been all day.

Somehow, we survived the week with only one major and one minor mishap. The major was that the nine-month-old twins had never had "table food" just "baby food." We collectively decided now is the time to introduce table food. Corn was the vegetable of choice – you got it- pink diarrhea - times two all over my mother's celery colored shag carpeting. The pink was from Pepto-Bismol. The minor mishap was when Mattie's wig got full of ants.

We all returned home to continue our lives of adventure, mundane or not.

Forward Sixteen Years to 1988...

Jerri, Casey, Lynda, Phoebe Ann and I made up the trip roster. Lynda was another sorority sister and Phoebe Ann was a friend of all.

We decided to go back to the beach for a week of "fun in the sun." Phoebe Ann was the driver of Casey's ugly brown van with gold stripes down the side. She was the designated driver, and we were the designated drinkers. We were supposed to leave at noon for the twelve-hour drive but did not get out of town until five p.m. Phoebe Ann drove and we snacked, sang, laughed, and did the "do you remember this?" and drank. Everything was good until we stopped in north Florida to get gas. The gas station was located a few miles from a small town on the Sewanee River where Lynda had lived with an abusive husband. The stop triggered a panic attack. After assuring Lynda that she was safe and we would keep her safe, we continued the drive. We arrived shortly after sunup, unloaded and crashed. I was awakened by Lynda tugging on my arm saying, "Petie wake up." (Petie was my college nickname). I struggled awake. Lynda was having another panic attack. I tried my best to calm her down, but, no go.

All the others were already on the beach. This was before cell phones. Lynda would not physically let go of me, so we had to go down to the beach to get help. She and I crossed the front yard, cheek-to-cheek with Lynda holding on to me with a near death grip. I explained to the girls we needed to take Lynda to the hospital. Back across the beach and across the front yard, Lynda was still cheek-to-cheek to the outdoor shower, which is where I wet her down, fully clothed. The trip to the hospital was not uneventful. We were in a construction zone and the van was on fumes. Phoebe Ann was driving, Lynda was in the passenger seat and I was sitting on the arm rest because Lynda still had a death grip on me We decided if the van ran out of gas we would commandeer the car behind us. We arrived and I took Lynda into the emergency room and explained she was having a heart attack. Three hours later the doctor said he had never treated anyone who had "olives in their blood work."

We returned to the beach. On arrival, Jerri said, "We have to go back to the hospital because Casey had tripped over the dishwasher door and hurt her ankle." Back to the hospital we went. Somehow, we made it to the next day. We had been on the beach and were returning to the house when Phoebe Ann meant to kick water on us from a small pool of water when she misjudged and kicked the sand instead of the water and hurt her ankle. We refused to take her to the hospital and put her in the recliner with a bag of frozen peas on her poor injured ankle. We did, however, go rent her some crutches.

We entertained ourselves with stories about the sailors on the Russian trawler anchored in front of the house. Jerri was in love with one of the sailors. The stories changed each day. We played cards and board games – always betting and always cheating. We had gymnastics exhibitions in the middle of the living room floor. I do not remember us going out. I think we were just too lazy to get dressed. We made a scrapbook with stupid pictures.

The ride back to Knoxville was uneventful. Sands and Times do change!

McPolio Shot

Nancy and I spent the night at Saundra's. It was our senior year in high school, and I cannot remember if it was Fall of 1957 or Spring of 1958 but it was time for another Polio shot.

Saundra's parents had already gone to work, and we were getting ready for school. Saundra was in the bathroom, and I was sitting on the kitchen counter with my feet in the sink. The health department was coming to the school to give Polio shots. We were to take a series of three shots, and I could not remember if I still needed a shot. I asked Nancy to call the health department and ask how many shots I had taken. (Note; Nancy, always, when reading aloud in class or speaking with a stranger, would assume a fancy way of speaking.)

My name is Patti McPeters. Keep in mind that I am seated on the kitchen counter with many feet in the sink. Nancy called the health department and in her fancy voice said, "can you tell me how many Peters Patti McPolio has had?" She repeated this the second time and then yelled "OH, shit" and slammed down the phone.

I told both Nancy and Saundra "one word of this and you are dead people." Of course, our tail-ends had not hit the front door of the school until everybody had heard.

To this day, ever so occasionally, I will run into somebody who says "there is Patti McPolio."

The Halos

Halos at Prom, 1958

Halos was our social club in high school. Our school was a small, rural school on the east side of the county and was the depository for any teacher no other school would take. We were aware that the larger city schools had more opportunities than we did. One of these was social clubs. We did not have one, so we made our own and called it the Halos. (I have no idea why we named the club the Halos). Our song was "You are My Special Angel" and our colors were Pink and Black. We had ten members, Saundra Niall, Nancy Clift, Nancy Cobb, Kaye Turbyville, Kay Maples, Katie Davis, Charlotte Bates, Pollie Scott, Virginia Hankins and me, Patti McPeters.

Each of us was either a basketball player or a cheerleader. Basketball was the only girl sport but football and basketball used cheerleaders. Which reminds me of a basketball trip, in the winter, to a small religious boarding school for a game. The girls always played before the boys. At this school we had to share the locker room with our boys. When we returned to the locker room after our game the boys had gone through our personal items, i.e. panties and bras. We needed to do "pay back" to get back at the boys. So we did...it was really cold outside...ice on the inside of the windows on the bus, cold. Our solution was to dip their whitey-tighteys in the commode.

Luncheon at Chesapeake's, 2022

All the boys, except one, left their wet underwear in the locker room. The one was Cecil Spencer and he brought his to the bus on a coat hanger and hung it out of the bus window and of course this caught the coach's attention. Nothing happened to the boys who started this whole mess but the coach told all us girls that we had to replace the boys' underwear. So we did...each of us bought a new pair, dyed them pastel colors and sewed lace on the butt part. The boys practiced in theirs and Cecil still has his.

The Halos would have slumber parties and stay up all night talking. We loved to go to Nancy Cobb's house. It was a big log house on the river, that had a two-way fire place from the living room to the bedroom. If we went to bed, three in bed and six on the floor in the living room.

Our only dress-up function was the Prom. This was really a big deal to each of us because it only happened once each year. I do not remember us doing anything charitable. Just doing the "go along...get along thing." To belong to something. As of this writing, Charlotte is deceased (dead sounds so final) and Katie is sick. Two years ago we had a luncheon at Chesapeake's and one month ago we went to the dedication of the Carter Elementary Lunch Room named for Saundra Naill. Amazing that most of us are still here sixty-seven years later.

*The Halos at the dedication of the Carter Elementary
School cafeteria, 2024*

The Wedding

Cecil was our class president and Ginny was a Halo. Cecil's wife and Ginny's husband had died. The two of them spent time talking at our class reunion. Cecil went back to Indiana but he and Ginny continued their conversation by phone. Time passes and Cecil moves in with Ginny here in East Knox County. They were living in sin but the only people it bothered were the two of them because none of us cared. We, Ruth Ann, Saundra and I decided they would feel better about themselves if they were married. So, we decided to give them a Wedding. And we did.

Ruth Ann Trying on Ginny's Wedding Gown

135

I cannot remember having more fun planning an event. Ruth Ann and I went wedding shopping at Hobby Lobby where we bought everything for a well-turned-out wedding. We even bought Ginny's wedding gown at Hobby Lobby which consisted of a 6' by 3' piece of white lacey fabric. We cut a hole in the center and pulled it down over Ginny's head. Instant wedding gown. After Ruth Ann and I bought everything, we went to Saundra's to show her our purchases which included a top hat for the preacher, Bissell, boutonnières for the men in the wedding party....... flowers for the bride and a guest book. Also, that is when we cut the hole in the fabric and pulled it down over Ruth Ann's head to see if it would work as we had envisioned. It did. The ceremony was held around Saundra's pool. Karen Hill brought her keyboard and provided live music. There were thirty guests, and we had a potluck.

Ginny

This was a big surprise to Cecil and Ginny because they knew nothing about a wedding. They just thought they were going to a Saturday night Potluck at Saundra's. We explained that them that living in sin was not a problem for any of us but knew they felt a little uncomfortable.

Cecil and Ginny's Wedding Ceremony

Our wedding was so successful and so much fun that a few weeks later they called a real preacher and really got married in the eyes of God and the laws of the State of Tennessee.

P.S. We did not invite any of their children because we did not know if they would think it as much fun as we did....

CERTIFICATE **Of** PARTICIPATION

Jenny and Cecil

is thanked for their phenomenal participation on

TEAM CARTER

PRESENTED BY: *Class of '58*

ON THIS DAY: *September 8, 2017*

Wedding Certificate

Trentville

Trentville was the tiny neighborhood in East Knox County where I grew up. In the late 1940s and early 1950s, my brother Doug and I lived with Granny and Grandad McPeters across the road from Lyons Creek Baptist Church and next door to the Trentville Cemetery. Our neighbors to the north were the cemetery and to the south were the Walkers. The Walkers were a big family. Mr. And Mrs. Walker and their four children lived side-by-side down Strawberry Plains Pike, and across the road were the Maynards. The three families were the Walkers, McPeters and the Maynards.

Doug, Patti, and Carolyn 1946

Our playground was anywhere outside but for an adventure we would take a can of pork n'beans and crackers and stay all day in the woods. The woods were on the other side of the cemetery and there was a creek that ran through it which allowed us to be good and dirty when we came home. We had to walk through the cemetery to get to the woods. We also played in the cemetery. In fact, we learned to smoke sitting behind tombstones. We rolled up newspaper and that is what we smoked. There were marble slabs on a few of the graves and that is where we learned to roller skate and tap dance. I had to walk through the cemetery to get milk at Miss Gertie's. I loved going to Miss Gerties because she always had sweet potatoes warming on her wood cook stove. Sometimes I would stay too late and have to walk back in the almost dark…through the cemetery.

We were always welcome at the Walkers. Junior and Mildred Walker got the first television set. All of us neighborhood kids were allowed to come to their house on Saturday morning and watch "snow" on the TV until wrestling came on at 11:00 a.m. There were no television stations anywhere near us and the station we watched came out of Chicago. We sat quietly in the floor and silently watched the snow and test pattern. What a marvel! What a wonder! How did this work? We could hardly see the wrestling men because of the "snow" but it was magical.

The Walker family built a swimming pool behind Junior and Mildred's house. They dug the hole, mixed and poured the concrete, installed a diving board and ladders. One summer they invited all the neighborhood kids to take swimming lessons, and I was the teacher. Everything when smoothly until the last day, which was "test day." I used the Red Cross swimming guide to teach skills, and this was the "test." We were just getting ready to begin class when I noticed a boy in the pool who seemed to be struggling. I watched until I saw he really was in trouble. I jumped in and pulled him over to the ladder and I calmly got out of the pool, trying not to draw any attention to him. Somebody always brought me a quart fruit jar of sweet tea. I calmly picked up the jar to take a drink, but my hands were shaking so badly I never got it to my mouth. I tried this three times and just gave up. So much for being calm."

On school mornings my cousin, Carolyn, Doug and I would walk down to Gary Walker's house next door, so we could all walk to school together. If you lived less than one mile from school, the bus would not pick you up and we lived just a little short of a mile, so we walked. We always had to wait on Gary because his mother fed him his breakfast. We stood and watched as she fed him and called him "Guykie." (Funny, the things you remember).

The Maynards' goats got out and ate my Granny's shrubs. Not cool, but these are the things that make life a life. We all survived, grew into productive adults and most of us are still here.

141

Patti and her brother Doug

A Water Extravaganza

The Carter Swim Club presents QUIET VILLAGE with Henry Mancini, August 28, 1969.

A message from the Director:

It has been my pleasure for the last few weeks to work with the Youth of this community. They have worked long, tiresome, late hours, and the fact that only a few have ever seen a water show made no difference.

They were willing to work and practice anywhere from 8:00 am to 11:00 pm. Be proud as you watch the show this evening and pay attention not to the quality of performance but to the quality of performers.

This is community spirit in action and I am proud to have been included.

Sincerely,
Patti M. Smith

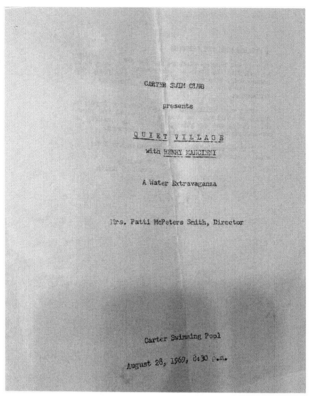

Carter Swim Program 1

This information is taken from the program of the show. Here is a lineup of numbers, performers and support staff.

QUIET VILLAGE
Susan Cox, Marsha Dalton, Carolyn Bell, Suzanne Smith, Becky Nipper, Laura Walker, Joy Pollard, Karen McNutt, Pam Gibson, Ginger Moreland, Terry Swaggerty, Becky Cowan.

DEAR HEART
Alice Forgety and Mike Walker, Audrey Willard and Rick
Walker, Molly Chesney and David Ownby

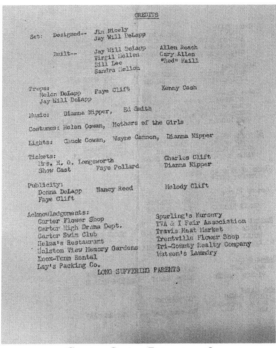

Carter Swim Program 2

ELEPHANT WALK
Karen McNutt, Laura Walker, Joy Pollard, Marcia Dalton,
Susan cox, Vickie Morrell, Terry Swaggerty, Suzanne Smith

DAYS of WINE and ROSES
Melody Clift

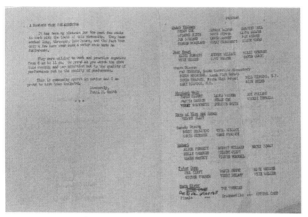

Carter Swim Program 3

COMEDY DIVING
Buddy Browning, Chris Hiscock, Bill Hiscock, Chris Hiscock, Gary Hiscock

HATARI
Alice Forgety, Audrey Willard, Becky Cowan, Molly Chesney, Melody Clift, Karen McNutt, Vickie Morrell

PETER GUNN
Hal Clift, David Ownby, Rick Walker, Victor Turner, Terry Delapp, Mike Walker

Note: The boys were told that they would be wearing tights because during a surface dive all you would see is teenage big feet and hairy legs so I explained that the tights would give a nice smooth look. The boys were horrified and were allowed to not wear tights. I told the boys that I understood that if this would ruin their manhood that they should not wear tights. After a moment they decided that they could do this and then proceeded to just about "silly" themselves to death.

MOON RIVER
Debra Morrell and Tom Thurman
Note about this number: Debra's mother had made Tom a gold lame tank top and Debra a one-piece gold lame suit. During the number Tom lifted Debra into a back layout and turned slowly around. As Tom was turning it dawned on Debra's mom that she had only basted the crotch of the suit. Can you imagine waiting for the number to be over? All ended well...thank goodness.

FINALE: DREAMSVILLE, ENTIRE CAST
SET DESIGN by Jim Nicely and Jay Will DeLapp and built by Jay Will DeLapp, Virgil Mellon, Bill Lee, Saundra Mellon, Allen Roach, Gary Allen, "Red" Naill.

PROPS by Helen DeLapp, Jay Will DeLapp, Faye Clift, Kenny Cash
MUSIC by Dianna Nipper and Ed Smith
COSTUMES by Helen Cowan, Mothers of the Girls
LIGHTS by Chuck Cowan, Wayne Cannon, Dianna Nipper
TICKETS. By Mrs. H.G. Longsworth and Charles Clift
SHOW CAST by Faye Pollard and Dianna Nipper
PUBLICITY by Donna DeLapp, Nancy Reed, Melody Clift, Faye Clift

ACKNOWLEDGEMENTS: Carter Flower Shop, Carter High Drama Dept., Carter Swim Club, Helma's Restaurant, Holston View Memory Gardens, Knox-Tenn Rental, Lay's Packing Company, Spurling's Nursery, TVA & I Fair Association, Travis meat Market, Trentville Flower Shop, Tri-County Realty Company, Watson's Laundry and LONG-SUFFERING PARENTS.

This was quite an undertaking for all of us. The Cowan family, owners of Knox-Tenn donated bleachers, towers and spotlights which made us look professional (sort of). The set also gave us the look of "we have a show" ... not just swimmers. When it was all over, we were proud of ourselves. Like I already said, "glad I was included."

Carter Water Show

Moonshine... The Elixir of the Mountains

This happened on October 1, 2024. My friends Kay and Howard had been to a meeting in Indianapolis and attended a party on Saturday night. They returned to Knoxville and on Monday morning they both woke up with COVID... I talked to Kay this morning and she did not need anything, but I told her, "You need Moonshine." It will cure anything. I went to the local Moonshine store and bought chocolate flavored Moonshine. I love it. I was standing in line to pay, and a man was in front of me and asked me about my dog, Petie. I told him she was a shelter dog and where I got her and how long I had had her.

I had my charge card out to pay but there was no product on the counter. The cashier said the man had paid for it because he liked that I had rescued Petie. I immediately turned around and saw a woman ready to pay with her card and I said "Wait, don't do that." I think she thought I was going to attack her because I was on my way around the counter. I said, "I will pay for your order," and she said, "it is $80," and I said, "I will pay $30." She said, "I have to do something," and I said, "I am writing a book, and you can buy it in December." She told me her friend owned a bookstore in the 100 Block of Gay Street, where I lived for twenty-seven years and I told her I had already been there and asked to do a book signing and they told me it would cost $250. She said, "I will take care of it." Is that not a feel-good story? We will see if that works out.

This reminded me of the first time I drank Moonshine in 1960, when my roommate was Marcia at MTSU in Middle Tennessee. She came home with me one weekend and we had nothing to do so we drove to Douglas Lake. While we were there, she mentioned that her daddy wanted her to be in every state before she went to college but she had never been to North Carolina. Asheville was only two hours away, so we decided to drive her over into North Carolina. This was before I-40 and we were driving on two lane curvy mountain roads. We were inside Carolina, going down the mountain when I heard a big clunk and looked back, and a big piece was bouncing down the road behind us. We coasted down the mountain and came to a tiny service station with one pump. We stopped and explained that my car had lost a part. The car was an English convertible and of course they had no parts for any car, much less an English Hillman. So, Marcia called her boyfriend in Knoxville to come pick us up. We had about a three hour wait and nobody knew where we were, not even us.

I remember sitting on top of a big stack of tires and the young man at the service station asked if we would like some Moonshine. Well of course we could not be rude and turn down hospitality. The next thing I remember is being lifted off the ground. Apparently, I was on my way up the hill to the outhouse when I surrendered to the effects of the Moonshine. Her boyfriend came and drove us back to Knoxville. The next thing I had to do was explain to my mother that my English Hillman Convertible was in North Carolina, and had to be repaired and returned to Knoxville. I have often said that "it is not easy being me," but this time it was: "it is not easy being my mother." This explains why I said, "MOONSHINE is the Elixir of the Mountains.

Miscellaneous

Recent Yesterdays

This afternoon I was trying to think of something that happened yesterday and when I remembered—— it had happened this morning.

Fourth of July in Deadwood, South Dakota

The filing cabinet in my head seems to be choosing wrong file folders more often..... When I was in business I never was much of a filer...... stacks seemed to work. The biggest drawback from using stacks instead of filing is stacks get shuffled around...... you know like: not putting pimentos in pimento cheese...... or when discussing turkey gravy and it just comes out as turkey syrup .... Nothing hurts or feels bad— just rearranging the stacks...... but on the other hand, going through files until you find the correct word that has mis-filed....never have been very good at spelling anyway——— just seems to me that the whole reason for spelling is communication. So, if you can "spell-at-it"....... that is good enough.

Giraffe House in Nairobi, 2012

So, looks as if resent yesterdays are okay....... Just needs to work for the moment.

Max and Patti celebrate Patti's 83rd birthday at the Pub Crawl in Dublin, Ireland, 2023.

Max and Patti have a beverage in Lagos, Portugal, 2023.

The Mountains in Houston

The mountains in Houston are concrete...... amazing... some of them are very high and I am afraid to look because other vehicles around me are going fast and it would not take much for me to go flying off the concrete mountain into a concrete abyss.... maybe after more experience or riding as a passenger I will have a more scenic view and appreciation of the downtown mountains.

What makes the concrete mountains so interesting is that the land is flat...as in "flitter flat." If I were to name this mountain range, I would call it the Southwest Downtown Concrete Mountain Range or SWDCMR or maybe the East Texas Downtown Concrete Mountain Range or ETDCMR...but my favorite is the Lone Star Downtown Concrete Mountain Range or LSDCMR.

Once you descend the mountain to the flat there is a special lane for changing your mind. The sign says, "Turn Around Only." Don't you think it is interesting that in greater Houston, a population of over seven million, that there are so many people who want or need to change their mind? I do. The Greater Houston population in 2018 was 6,997,384 and in 2020 had increased to 7,122,240. Lord knows what it is in 2022. Another thing I have noticed about the Greater Houston inhabitants is that they are mostly reclusive. Haven't met any neighbors except for one. Her name is Jane and she was out for her morning walk and I waved her down to ask something....... can't remember what, but anyway... I found out she has lived in this mature neighborhood for thirty-two years and doesn't know anybody here. She worked for thirty years, retired and now volunteers at her church. I invited her to go to the fifty plus get-together at the clubhouse but she declined. Over seven million people is a lot of people and makes me wonder, since nobody wants to know anybody, how do they multiply?

Patti at Waffle House, Spring, Texas

Acknowledgments

To each of you who have worked to help put these tales together, I thank you. To each of you who were part of the tales that shaped my life, I thank you. I am thankful for growing up in East Knox County and Strawberry Plains and so proud to have been included in the revitalization of the 100 Block of Gay Street in downtown Knoxville.

Self Portrait, 1985

Made in the USA
Columbia, SC
02 December 2024

47208060R10087